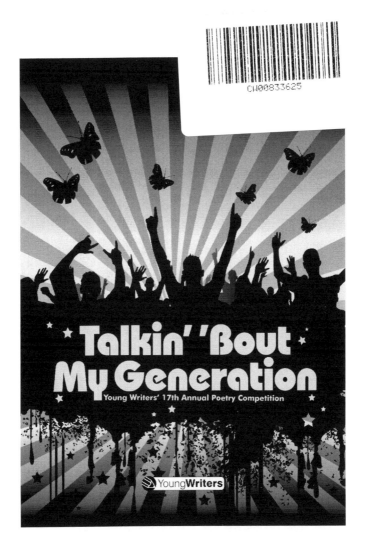

Talkin' 'Bout My Generation
Young Writers' 17th Annual Poetry Competition

YoungWriters

Southern England
Edited by Michelle Afford

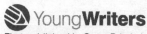

First published in Great Britain in 2008 by:
Young Writers
Remus House
Coltsfoot Drive
Peterborough
PE2 9JX
Telephone: 01733 890066
Website: www.youngwriters.co.uk

SB ISBN 978-1 84431 481 2

Foreword

This year, the Young Writers' *Talkin' 'Bout My Generation* competition proudly presents a showcase of the best poetic talent selected from thousands of up-and-coming writers nationwide.

Young Writers was established in 1991 to promote the reading and writing of poetry within schools and to the young of today. Our books nurture and inspire confidence in the ability of young writers and provide a snapshot of poems written in schools and at home by budding poets of the future.

The thought, effort, imagination and hard work put into each poem impressed us all and the task of selecting poems was a difficult but nevertheless enjoyable experience.

We hope you are as pleased as we are with the final selection and that you and your family continue to be entertained with *Talkin' 'Bout My Generation Southern England* for many years to come.

Contents

Ben Collier   1

Brooklands Middle School, Leighton Buzzard
Roksana Szymanska (11)   2

De La Salle College, Jersey
Kean Mutter (11)   2
Jack Bailhache (11)   3
George Queree (11)   3
Charlie Eddie (11)   4
Oliver McBoyle (11)   4
Benjamin Pickersgill (16)   5

Ferndown Upper School, Ferndown
Charlotte Durling (15)   6
Diana Nelson (14)   6
Gemma Bentley (14)   7
Paul Roots (15)   7
Ruxandra Blidaru (14)   8
Johnathan Hughes (15)   9
Leah Charman (15)   10
Victoria Aldridge (15)   11
Chloe Bufton (14)   12
Stephen Male (15)   13
Fiona Richardson (14)   13
Alex Camp (14)   14
Rebecca Mole (15)   14
Aaron Robb (15)   15
Charlotte Bateman (15)   15
Sammie Brebner (14)   16
Beth Pharoah (14)   17
Chrissie Bacon (15)   17
Dan Cooper (14)   18
Deborah Quartey (14)   19
Taylor-Jade Hayward (14)   20
Jessie Butler (15)   21
Katie Libby (14)   22
Matt Francis (14)   23

Hannah Wells (14) 24
Daniel Tovey (14) 25
Alex Pook-Leary (14) 26
Marcus Still (15) 27
Dominic Fountaine (15) 28
Charlotte Balston (14) 28
Harriet Whiting (15) 29
Melissa Ingleton (14) 29

Guernsey Grammar School, St Andrews
Kasey Watson (12) 30
Katie Fallaize (17) 31
Chloe Norman (13) 32
Emilia Still (12) 32
Nathan Hazzan (12) 33
Clarice Parrott (12) 33
David Campbell (12) 34
Jessica Savident (12) 35
Heather Ewert (12) 36

Hautlieu School, Jersey
Ellie Perchard (15) 37
Sarah Gouyette (15) 38

Holyport Manor School, Holyport
Breffni Potter (15) 39
Richard Creffield (15) 40
Robert Barker (14) 40
Jamie Hepburn (13) 41
Ben Shepherdly (15) 41
Adam James Potter (14) 42
David Harber (13) 42
Sabina Nilsson (15) 43
Gagandeep Juttla (15) 43
Jamie Lloyd (16) 44
Sam Peacock (15) 44

Le Rocquier School, St Clement
Aimee Boissiere (11) 45
Daniel Heaven (11) 45

Stefan Le Marquand (15)   46
Raoul Crosby (12)   47
Danielle Le Verdier (11)   48
Audrey Bois (12)   48
Charlotte Turner (11)   49
Matthew Martin (14)   49
Catherine Richards (13)   50
Connie Lopez-Rubio (14)   50
Elvio Da Silva (13)   51

Lytchett Minster School, Poole
Yazmin Farasat (13)   51
Emma Milner (14)   52
Pippa Woods (13)   53
Jade Knight (13)   54

Mullion School, Helston
Thomas McCabe (12)   54
Charlotte Lawlor (12)   55
Lowenna Trimble (12)   56
Simone Hawkings (12)   57
Charlotte Roberts (12)   58

St Bernard's Convent School, Slough
Bethany Noble (13)   59

St Osmund's CE Middle School, Dorchester
Fern Matthews (12)   60
Robbie Ward & Will Youngs   60
Ellie Schamroth (12)   61
Ben Killian & Steven Kelley (12)   61
Kathryn Flint (12)   62
Katie Andrew (12)   63
Emily Bate (12)   64
Kathrine Thompson-Ward (12)   65
Hilary Hansford (11)   65
Tom Whiter (11)   66
Alice Dodd (12)   67
Ashleigh Purvey   68
Luke Doherty (13)   69

James Ashington (12)	69
Joe Rutter (12)	70
Kerry Gorham (12)	70
Kieran Smith (12)	71
Max Warren (12)	71
Becky Walsh (12)	72
Pascal Chukwudozie Anyanjo (12)	72
Jack Merriott (12)	73
Ollie Sohawon (12)	73
Jasmine Cottrell (11)	74
Freddie Stacey (12)	74
Lauren Coffey (12)	75
Chloe Jefferies (12)	76
Emily Diaz & Laura Caines (12)	77
Poppy Cranswick & Rebecca Diaz (12)	78
Juliette Bone (12)	79
Amy Bradford (12)	80
Jessica Element (11)	81
Matthew Hurley (12)	82
Annabel Macklin (11)	83
Carina Clark (12)	84
Georgia Viller (12)	85
Helen Carter (12)	86
Jahlemn David (12)	86
Evan Cumber (12)	87
Connor Gould (12)	87
Matthew Hart (12)	88
Ellie Clark (12)	88

Sandhurst School, Sandhurst

Louise Williamson (15)	89

Shaftesbury School & Sports College, Shaftesbury

Sam Alford (12)	89
Lianne Hooper (17)	90
Matthew Crumpler (17)	91
Robert Broughton (16)	92
Gareth Way (13)	93
Tim Hardiman (15)	94
Jodie Robinson (15)	95

Tom Whitfield (17)   96
Frances Bathurst (13)   97

The Emmbrook School, Wokingham
Josie Brownlee (11)   98
Alex Harvey (11)   99
Danielle Murray (12)   100
Hazel Gambles (11)   101
Rachel Cox (11)   102
Oliver Johnson (11)   103
Laura Carter (13)   104
Megan Shillibier (11)   105
Matthew Farndon (12)   106
Harry Beasley (11)   107
Katherine Stubbs (11)   108
Anna Phillips (11)   109
Jessica Phipps (11)   110
Elliott Jones (11)   111
Nathan Onraet-Wells (13)   112
Nadia Glover (12)   113
Ellie Horne (11)   114
Ben Brown (12)   115
Becky Morrell (14)   116
Becca Tizzard (11)   117
Mark Brown (13)   118
Amy Allpress (14)   119
Rachael Skinner (13)   120
Ellie Phillips (11)   121
Casey Ward (11)   122
Katriona Gardner Whitney (11)   123
Liam Pietrasik (11)   124
Samantha Barnett (11)   125
Stephanie Jacqueline Kent (12)   126
Mitchell Webb (11)   127
Aaron Scicluna (12)   128
Sarah Colbourn (11)   128
Josh Pymble (11)   129
Maximillion Crowhurst (12)   129
Will Shillibier (13)   130
Tom Peterson (11)   131
Natasha Keane (13)   132

The Grange School, Christchurch

Bronwyn Annetts (12)	132
Jack Frampton (11)	133
Kiera Barton (11)	133
James Baron (11)	133
Jade Rowing (11)	134
Annie Malla (11)	134
Katie Sida (11)	135
Peter Wedge (12)	135
Alice Burton (11)	136
Chelsea Heanes (12)	136
Rhys Daniels (11)	137
Callum Gooch (11)	137
Jordan Perry (11)	138
Zac Tilsed (11)	138
Eden Warne (12)	138
Stacey Murphy (12)	139
Lauren Hood (12)	139
Levi Ridealgh (11)	139

The Ladies' College, St Peter Port

Amy Stenner (12)	140
Eden Staples (12)	141
Sunaina Reddy (12)	142
Erin Renouf (12)	143
Sophie Morellec (12)	143
Laura Stoddart (12)	144
Ellie Taylor (12)	145
Elizabeth Reynolds (12)	146
Laura Oxburgh (12)	147
Izzie Sheil (12)	148
Samantha Carter (12)	149
Louise Vivian (12)	150
Natalie Hadley (12)	150
Abigail Corbet (12)	151
Rebekah Fant (12)	151
Nicky Bourne (12)	152
Flinty Bane (12)	153
Emma Baxendale (12)	154
Freddie Best (12)	155
Amber Buckingham (12)	156

Charlotte Brooksbank (12)   157
Helen Monachan (12)   158
Sian Brodrick (13)   159
Dannie Jones (12)   160
Kirsty Bynam (12)   161
Evie Domaille (12)   162
Laura Corbet (13)   163
Lydia Collas (12)   164
Rhiannon Carys Jones (12)   165
Lauren Buckingham (12)   166
Jessica Fiore (12)   166
Elinor Freestone (12)   167
Emily Martel-Dunn (12)   167
Rosie Davis (13)   168
Abi Howard (12)   169
Francesca Bachelet (12)   169
Alice Davis (13)   170
Lisa Marquand (12)   171
Kate Friedlaender (12)   172
Emily Maindonald (12)   173

Uplands School, Poole

Ollie Shrimpton (16)   173
Aston McCarthy (12)   174
Aimée Guichard (13)   174
Lillie Cohen (14)   175
Otis Ooi (14)   175
Bianca Arden (14)   176
Jack Fuller (14)   177
Jack Webster (14)   178
Anoush Fard (15)   178
Shadman Chowdhury (15)   179
William Smith (15)   179
Frank Morley (11)   180
James Stone (15)   181
Byron Russell (15)   182
Hollye McKenzie (15)   183
Ben Rogers (15)   184
Robert Kerr (15)   185
Daniel Giles (15)   186
Piers Anderson (12)   186

Max Ooi (12)	187
Oliver Jagger (11)	187
Rebecca Baxendale (12)	188
Sam Harbord (12)	188
Pavlos North (12)	189
Daniel Sharland (12)	189
Chris Brewer (12)	190
Katie Pearce (12)	190
Lucy Carter (11)	191
Emily Condie (11)	191
Bethany Williams (15)	192
Andrew Power (12)	192
Wesley Glover (14)	193
Cassidy Ooi (12)	193
Beth Dooley (11)	194
Emma Smith (12)	194
Alasdair Burn (12)	195
Matt Holland (12)	195
Jeremy Bond (14)	196
George Fullerton (15)	196
Jaina Vithana (11)	197
Dan Pritchard (15)	197
Toby Adams (14)	198
Tom Evans (14)	199
Liam Meakin (12)	199
Alex Wyer (11)	200
Jonathan Summerell (14)	200
Lauren Talbot (12)	201
Roseanna Au (12)	201
Megan Hallowes (12)	202
Oliver Gristwood (12)	202
Lauren Bungay (12)	203
James Heslington (11)	203
Jake Redrupp (12)	204
Ariana Woolrych (12)	205
Robert Bell (12)	206
Anthony Skilton (16)	206
Eileen Stone (15)	207
Savannah Townsend (13)	207
Casey Fullerton (12)	208
Liam Mather (14)	208
William Evans (13)	209

Oliver Williams (15)   209
Sophie Amanda Pearce (14)   210
Ali Wilson (15)   211
Joseph Krolski (14)   212
Jack Abrahams (14)   213
Edward Parker (13)   214
Tom Hawkins (15)   215
Georgie Rowbrey (13)   216
Melissa Ward (13)   217
Joanna Tonge (13)   218
Tishco Gurdji (14)   219
James Marlowe   219
India De Silva Jeffries (13)   220
Katherine Charman (13)   221
Rob Booth (13)   222
Will Brown (15)   223
Timothy Johnson (15)   224
Toby Khalife   225
Jamie Everett (12)   226
Peter Jeff (14)   227

The Poems

Here To Stay

When I'm gone don't blame yourself
I had a good time out on the shelf.
I lived life well, oh so well,
But you will cry, I can tell.
But if you cry you will not see
And will be unable to remember me.
So have a laugh and have some fun
And remember the good about your son.
I may be gone but I'm always here,
You won't lose me easily my dear!
But I hope you sort your hair
Cos it's a mess (I say cos I care).
Worry yourself about things like this,
So that people you won't miss.
But I'm here now and for many a year,
So everybody please don't fear.
I love you all I need to say
And more important I'm here to stay.

Ben Collier

I Am A Book

I am a book, I talk and walk,
And at night I just wish I were free,

People rip my pages,
And keep me in cages,

Although I don't have many friends
I have feelings and that hurts,

People think I'm dam,
But I just love jam,

My owner is a bully,
I hate him,
Wouldn't you?

Oh please, I just want to be free!

Roksana Szymanska (11)
Brooklands Middle School, Leighton Buzzard

The Walk

Down Barking Dog Lane,
Past a street with a boat,
Clouds rushing by,
Sometimes it rains.

Up the new lane,
Past a field with a car,
Aeroplanes hovering.

Down Skateboard Road,
Past the shop with the cat,
Clouds form shapes,
With reflecting windows.

Kean Mutter (11)
De La Salle College, Jersey

My Dog Mac

Mac is a lively little Westie,
That runs around like a bull,
He digs up the grass,
Then buries our shoes in a hole.

What Mac really likes,
Is lying on his back,
Sticks his legs in the air,
And I give him a belly rub.

When he sees you,
He will run towards you,
Jumps up on you,
And licks you to death.

When he's in bed,
He closes his eyes,
Snores and kicks everywhere,
And that's him done for the day!

Jack Bailhache (11)
De La Salle College, Jersey

Rugby

Rugby is a fast and furious game,
Not for the faint-hearted,
It's a scrum, it's a maul, the ball has now gone,
Sliding through the mud and jumping in the air,
The ball has gone, but where?

George Queree (11)
De La Salle College, Jersey

If You Were A Car, What Car Would You Be?

Would you be . . .
Slick and shiny, built for speed
Old and battered, one of a breed

Tinted windows, black and green
Or roof down so you can be seen

Alloy wheels, flames of gold
Look at me, aren't I bold?

Heated seats, pop-up lights
All set to cruise through the night

Rusted tow bar and old roof rack
Battered trailer on the back (my dad's car)

Vintage style or modern looks
Get ideas from Clarkson's books

As long as you get from A to B
Your car sounds good enough to me

You could have an Aston Martin DB9
In my dreams it would be mine.

Charlie Eddie (11)
De La Salle College, Jersey

Ruby

Her face is as gold as a golden pyramid.
Her eyes are like a winter night when everything is switched off.
Her nose is like a burnt marshmallow.
Her ears are as pink as chewing gum.
Her tummy is as big as a Land Rover.
Her teeth are as sharp as a needle.
Her claws are as long as an HB pencil.
Her legs are as skinny as a twig.
Her tail is like a hairy sausage.

Oliver McBoyle (11)
De La Salle College, Jersey

An Ocean

Day by day the battle grows
as time goes by the oceans flow.

Every day the spears they lunge
and ocean waves begin to launch.

I feel the blow, it cuts down deep
it does not kill, but takes its toll
I feel the blood, I lose more and more
and so the soldier falls to the ground
accepting fate and lying down.

The oceans flow back and forth
they grow in strength as each one goes
faster and faster the oceans grow
the gripping torrent takes control.

Day by day the spears they pierce
cutting deep as they taste flesh
the soldier moans but carries on
as more blades strike and more blood flows.

The oceans grow and then they go
ready
for the next assault!

Benjamin Pickersgill (16)
De La Salle College, Jersey

Barriers

Saw it on the TV, they held nothing back.
And it looked so easy, I just had to have a crack.
Don't tell me that we can't, done it all before.
No one will care if I end up wanting more.
We've explored every inch, both far and near.
I've heard all the facts that I could ever want to hear.
I have tried every thrill, but I still want more.
Seen every sight, looked right down to the core.
We all need a meaning, we're all the same.
Take away its point and life is just a game.
Technology can do it for us, so don't even try.
But it burns up the planet, so we'll just sit and fry.
There aren't any barriers that are out of reach.
But the barriers there we just can't breach.
We're the generation with barriers and nowhere else to go.

Charlotte Durling (15)
Ferndown Upper School, Ferndown

One Heart

So many groups in just one place,
Not divided by colour and definitely not race,
Not the colour of their hair,
But the kind of clothes they wear.
Without noticing this has become daily routine,
Who would have thought it matters where you sit in the canteen?
The way you talk, the way you style your hair,
The small-mindedness is almost too much to bear,
How can people be so close yet so far apart?
We're all the same: one person, one world, one heart!

Diana Nelson (14)
Ferndown Upper School, Ferndown

Make Or Break

Everything I've ever wanted,
Everything I've worked for,
Could be destroyed within seconds . . .
If I don't get this right.

Working from dawn to dusk,
Fingers numb from cutting and pinning,
Eyes strained and bloodshot from sewing with precision.

If I get this right I could go to the top,
But it's easy in this business to be a total flop,
I'm aiming high fashion,
Not high street.
I want my clothes to be worn by Lily Cole not Lily Savage.

My whole life depending on a six-minute fashion show,
I take a sharp intake of breath as the music begins,
This is it . . .
           Make or break!

Gemma Bentley (14)
Ferndown Upper School, Ferndown

School

The school bell rings, break up the huddle
know where you're going so you're not in a muddle
if the teacher is late
don't be irate.

If he starts to diss
just take the piss
if the work is too borin'
you'll find yourself snorin'.

Before homework is set
try to make him forget
that today is Monday
our seriously fun day.

Paul Roots (15)
Ferndown Upper School, Ferndown

Deadly Flight

Once happy,
Flying high,
Now so scared
That I might die.

A shadow upon me
So dark and sly
Watching me as I
Blow dry.

You were quite polite
Not interrupting
One might say
You were even
Out hunting.

Hunting? What for
When you only
Had dinner at four?

Now you're hungry
Aggressive
But really
It's not like I'm
A digestive!

You reach
I fly
You smash
I cry.

I flew again
Lights went out
I got covered
By a cloud!

Then you crushed me
And I died
My insides
And my head
Were underneath
My leg.

Now I'm dead
Gone to bug heaven
It is quite cool
So thanks, to you.
You b*****d.

Ruxandra Blidaru (14)
Ferndown Upper School, Ferndown

Life Is War

Bullets blasting,
Blades piercing,
Fists beating.

Why is life like war?

Governments the hunters,
Citizens the hunted.

Why does life include war?

Grenades exploding,
Napalm burning,
Nukes vaporising,

Why has life got to be war?

Voices killing,
Innocence dying,
Crying is silent.

Why is life *war*?

Johnathan Hughes (15)
Ferndown Upper School, Ferndown

What Am I To Do?

What are you supposed to feel,
when your mother says she's OK,
but as you look into her eyes
tears are streaming down her face?

What are you supposed to feel,
when your father holds his fist up high,
and slams it down into her face,
as you hear her let out a cry?

How are you supposed to act,
when the next day everything is great,
but the night before, your father was a menace,
and filled with so much hate?

Where are you supposed to go,
when you know what will happen that night,
when you can't stand to be near the man you're supposed to love,
because he gives you such a fright?

How are you supposed to sleep,
when you've been told to go to bed,
and then starts the shouting and you hear a thud,
and you're sure it's his fist to her head!

Leah Charman (15)
Ferndown Upper School, Ferndown

Anathema

Mother always says the world just isn't right for you.
How can someone, so calm, gentle,
A quiet nature, you were smacked down with no compunction,
No guilt, no sorrow nor grief.

Concealed in a disguise that doesn't fit.
Revealed again but only to be desolate and persecuted,
By a forty-year-old ruffian, stuck in his ways.
Barbarian! She was clean for three months solid
Until your barricade of asceticism,
Subjected us to inescapable narcissistic pity.

This is your doing . . .
Her fair, pale skin tarnished with raw red cuts.
Her craving for approval, driven slowly to destruction.
Now look what you have made.
Now look how you have trained her.

Procreator. Predecessor.
Founder, creator, inventor.
Take this blame and tie the long, hellish cord
Of her ill-will around your neck.
Believe me it will weigh you down,
To the depths that you already command.

Victoria Aldridge (15)
Ferndown Upper School, Ferndown

Sweet Sacrifice

A life unlived
Forgotten by the world.
A face that hid behind the crowd.
Every day became the same,
That day replayed again and again.
Every morning she awoke,
A thousand thoughts running through her head.
She thought about the times gone by,
A thousand smiles
And a thousand lies
Just to cover up those tears they made her cry.
The tears that fell during those sleepless nights,
When she lay there knowing no one cared.
About a life so worthless,
A life lived in hope of death,
The hope that every day would come and leave and her time was
                                                    soon to pass,
But every day was lived in vain.
She fell asleep, she cried herself there,
Then awoke the next day.
Just another day,
Just another girl.
Just another lost cause in the world.
They watched her as she started losing grip,
Stared as she started to slip.
The rain pouring upon her as she took her one last breath
And tried to make what was only pathetic, as poetic as she could.
They looked into her eyes; this was them; what they had done.
Her time had come and they had bought it upon a silver platter.
This, was her sweet escape!

Chloe Bufton (14)
Ferndown Upper School, Ferndown

A Look At Life

Life is but a fleeting dream in the infinite blackness of sleep.
A breath of wind before the night.
A blink of the eye before the long waking day begins.
None can escape.
We bring nothing in and we can take nothing out.
There is but our allocation of breaths, nothing more, nothing less.
A lifetime can feel like an age but lasts but fractions of time.
None can escape.
Time is the one true constant ticking away, counting down
                                    towards our eventual end.
Some become rich, some poor, but in the end no one can stave
                                    off death.
Death is the most ruthless of entities, a harbinger of our
                                    continued mortality.
None can escape.
Life is but a fleeting glance.
A flash of lightning before the storm.
You can live a life of generous bounties or one of lasting seclusion.
But in the end none can escape.

Stephen Male (15)
Ferndown Upper School, Ferndown

Bullies Let Me

Cruel fate, set date
Bell rings, kids scream
Racing past, running fast
Silent cars, gear up.

Silent child, swinging round
Holding on, for what's gone
A little note, forced choke
His bodyweight, a heart pace.

The loose noose, a bit confused
Heavy rock, for the drop
Hidden tears, school fears
A laugh from those he fears.

Fiona Richardson (14)
Ferndown Upper School, Ferndown

No Escape

Making your way in the armoured car
Good, base isn't far
But then the air is rent apart
And suddenly you're in the heart,
The soul of the battle
All you can think of is the rattle
Of the gun firing upon you
Like predator on prey
That's all you can do, pray
Pray that you won't end up like them,
Those for whom this war will cost more than a leg and arm
But now it's all calm
Dare you take a peek
Or is that what they seek?
A target, that's you
So what to do?
No escape
All you can do is wait!

Alex Camp (14)
Ferndown Upper School, Ferndown

Image

To you it's all about fashion,
To us it's who we are,
We are all the light in the darkness,
We represent who we are.

Every person should be different,
Why should we all be the same?
Can't you accept we dress differently?
You look on us with shame.

Tell me why you think we're different?
We're all the same, don't you see?
Why must we fight over the clothes we wear,
Self-expression should be free.

Rebecca Mole (15)
Ferndown Upper School, Ferndown

Chains

Breaking my chains can be difficult
when people keep holding me back.
I just want to be individual
and step out of this deep pool of black.

Into the light of tomorrow,
that's where I want to be,
not caring about if I should show
the sheep that this is the real me.

Breaking my chains should be easy,
I have my whole future ahead.
Yet tangling vines wrap around me
and softly smother my head.

Too easy to give in and suffer.
Be strong and forget all the rest.
Breaking away from the others
is hard, but it is for the best.

Aaron Robb (15)
Ferndown Upper School, Ferndown

Tell Us

I'm too small,
She's too tall,
He's too fat,
They're too thin.
Our hair's not right,
Our clothes are wrong.
So tell us,
Who's left?

Charlotte Bateman (15)
Ferndown Upper School, Ferndown

Dying To Be Thin

Lying in a hospital bed,
Flicking through a magazine,
Hating all the models
And their beautiful frames.
She sits there,
Tears streaming down her face,
They will be back soon,
Trying, forcing her to eat,
She can't give up now,
They just don't understand
How important it is to look good,
How much it hurts to look in the mirror,
See herself.
People look at her in disgust and pity.
They just don't get it.
To eat is a sin, for her a curse.
She looks down at her arm,
Drip and wires puncture her skin.
If only she had the energy to tear them out.
To leave and to never come back.
The nurses try to comfort her,
Say she's pretty and slender.
All she sees is fat.
She hates being mistaken for an old lady,
Frail and brittle,
But what can she do?
Too weak to move,
Too proud to eat,
She'll die here
With the others,
All with the problem
They can't understand.

Soon they will realise

They were beautiful
            the way
                they were!

Sammie Brebner (14)
Ferndown Upper School, Ferndown

The Winner

She is my world
She carries me to victory
She is my best friend

Sat on her shoulders
Sat in the saddle
Wherever we go, we go as a team

We get through the hardest times together
She listens to everything
I can tell her anything
I look after her
She looks after me

She is my world
She carries me to victory
She is my best friend
She is my horse!

Beth Pharoah (14)
Ferndown Upper School, Ferndown

Who Knew?

Who knew what you were about to say?
Who knew what you were about to do?
Who knew why you were about to do it?
Who knew how?

Bang!

Who knows what you said?
Who knows what you did?
Who knows why you did it?
Who knows how?

Me.

I know.

And sleepless nights will follow me forever!

Chrissie Bacon (15)
Ferndown Upper School, Ferndown

The Way Of The Chav

Bike-lock sized, golden chains,
Fourteen Zs on the end of their names
Intimidating 'possies' and wannabes
Welcome to Dorset,
Out of safest countries . . .
. . . we're three.

Cheap Burberry and go-go Nike Shox
Two-pound trackies, tucked into their socks
Breath smelling like an ashtray
As sad it is, it's the 'Chav way'.

'Tis the way of the Chav,
The way they might have
'Tis the style of the Chav,
To pretend to act bad.

Working in 'Mackey Dees'
Ten years on, that's where they'll be.
Waiting to terrorise OAPS,
As sad as it sounds it's what they need!

'Chaving' bikes worth three hundred
'Where?' is what I ask, were they conjured
Afterwards, all his 'mates' he tells
Even though he sold it for ten
He ends up crying in a cell,
For a stolen PS2 he tried to sell.

Dan Cooper (14)
Ferndown Upper School, Ferndown

He's The One

He's the one I see,
He's the one I spot from the crowd.
He's the one I love.
He's the one that loves to see me in red.

Red isn't my favourite colour.
But I love him,
So I love red.
I forgive him when he dyes me red.

He's the one for me,
He's the one I love,
So what's the harm
In wearing a little red
Now and again?

Mum says he might be the one I love
And the one I say makes me happy,
But there's nothing enjoyable
About seeing me in hospital
Every weekend.

'Get help,' Mum says.
It's not right for him to hit you.

But what am I supposed to do
When he's the one?

Deborah Quartey (14)
Ferndown Upper School, Ferndown

Think Pink

Breast cancer is very common nowadays,
When we hear about it, we cry a tear,
But every one of us at FUS,
Can help one day a year,
By wearing pink on the 19th October,
And paying an amount of one pound,
We help the victims get through it,
And turn the frowns around.
There are many types of cancer,
Which are all difficult and expensive to cure,
But the money we raise at our school,
Can help a whole lot more.
We only have to do a little,
Which means so much to others,
The people who lose their loved ones,
Their fathers and their mothers.
It's not only women that get this,
It's common in men as well,
But not one knows that they will get it,
It's something you cannot tell.
Last year we did relay for life,
We can raise a whole lot more,
Come on, you will enjoy it,
It's fun, *not* a chore!
So when you come in on the 19th,
'The people I'm helping', just think,
By doing this little something . . .
Just think pink!

Taylor-Jade Hayward (14)
Ferndown Upper School, Ferndown

Life Holds A Bond

When you hold a baby in your arms,
She soothes and calms,
When you hold that little head near your own,
You know that you will never regret or moan,
That this baby is a sign of love,
From the Lord, up above.

When that baby has grown,
She brings happiness you have never known.
You may shout,
But without a doubt,
This child is such a precious gift,
The bond between you will never shift.

But now she is in her teenage years,
There are bound to be a few upset tears.
Even though you shout at each other,
The bond is still there undercover.

She is older now and with her own child.
A child all soft and mild,
Just like the one you held in your arms,
Who is now a mother who soothes and calms
Her child when he cries.
Your daughter who always tries

To keep that bond between mother and child,
Well and truly alive!

Jessie Butler (15)
Ferndown Upper School, Ferndown

Lost Memories

She stood, staring out the window,
Waiting for him to get back.
Day after day -
She thought about running away,
But where could she go?
He would surely just find her again.
She just wanted to be able to run and scream,
Anything - but stay like this. Trapped in a whole new world.
She had lost her life to him.
All those years.
All those memories - gone.
Just like that!

Now, looking back on all the past, all the memories,
At first, things had seemed like a good idea.
He had seemed like a nice man.
But now - looking back hurt her even more.
She had lost anyone who had really cared about her,
All because of him,
She was left alone,
Well almost. There was only him, one man,
But even he hated her so much as to dye her skin red.
So what could she do? Why couldn't the world just change?
Where could she go?
There was nowhere.

She would be strong enough to fight back . . . one day.

Katie Libby (14)
Ferndown Upper School, Ferndown

His Life In His Eyes

He went to see his friends, just the other day,
Abuse was thrown at him all along the way,
Gay, skater, goth, emo,
Is he any of these things? No!
Just because he wears different shirts,
Is that really any need to hurt?

He went to see his friends, just the other day,
He cared about nothing all along the way,
They hate his looks, is something wrong?
He likes what he wears;
He gets on with life,
But feels like no one cares.

He went to see his friends, just the other day,
He didn't want to do it, he just thought, *no way,*
No way am I going to lower myself,
And risk being bloodied and beaten and losing my health.
He walked away and didn't care,
That he had much longer hair.

He arrived at his friend's just the other day,
Angry, tired and wanting to hit the hay.
He was picked up that night,
After his terrible fright.
He was picked up later that night,
And never ever spoke of the fright!

Matt Francis (14)
Ferndown Upper School, Ferndown

Forever

As she sat there
Laughing with her friends
It suddenly hit her
It wouldn't be like this forever
They would grow
Move on
And it broke her heart
That time just couldn't stay still
And it could be like this forever
Where all we worried about
Were spots and boys
Where we could act like immature idiots
And not care
Summer days down the beach
And times where we laughed so much
Our tummies hurt
But then she realised
Although it wouldn't be like this forever
Her friends would always be there
And the memories
They would stay with her
Forever.

Hannah Wells (14)
Ferndown Upper School, Ferndown

Well?

Are you too afraid to be yourself?
Too sad, alone and insecure?
Would it affect your mental health,
If people found out who you were?

Do you hide behind your hair and clothes?
Your stupid sad identity?
Do you know all of the things I know?
You should be who you want to be!

So take off your mask and show your face,
No one wants to know or be a fake.

Do you feel down when you're alone?
Can't stand to face the ugly truth?
Do you hope and pray that no one knows
That there is something wrong with you!

Are you lost and alone out there?
Feel you have no place to turn?
If you be yourself, no one will care,
That's the lesson you must learn!

Daniel Tovey (14)
Ferndown Upper School, Ferndown

Fat Cat!

I have a cat,
and he's very fat,
he's round and ginger,
but his paws are flat.
He cannot walk,
and he cannot talk,
he rolls around,
I like to hug him,
but he doesn't hug back,
probably because
he's a silly fat cat.
He sits on my pillow,
and smells like wet hair,
he's 100% polyester,
I'm sure you're aware.
Fat cat's not alive,
He doesn't pounce, purr,
hiss or growl.
This is because he's from
the local shop . . . Asda!

Alex Pook-Leary (14)
Ferndown Upper School, Ferndown

Boy Racer

There he goes again -
Driving like a lunatic,
In his souped-up blue Saxo,
He thinks he's indestructible.

Three mates in the back,
One in the front,
50 Cent blares out
Of the windows.

After skipping the
Disk on two tracks,
He turns, and looks
To his friends in the back.

He turns back 'round,
Just in time to see
A cyclist mount his bonnet,
And sees her head enter
Through the windscreen!

Marcus Still (15)
Ferndown Upper School, Ferndown

Gothic Girl

At first he saw a messy girl,
A Gothic girl with hair about,
The clothes she wore, torn and ripped,
A face at which he could not look.

Her beauty shone across the park,
Inside the shadows the bowl,
He hid with feelings unknown,
He was in love but did not know.

For days they roamed around the town,
The flame-burst night of bonfire day,
All night they played and flirted,
And until the final moment . . .

The kiss,
That kiss,
That love-filled kiss,
It was only the beginning!

Dominic Fountaine (15)
Ferndown Upper School, Ferndown

Hide It

There is, no way
To describe it.
Everything we do,
Just tries to hide it.

No one understands,
The pain that could be caused,
But what if it,
It could be paused,
Would you want to try it?

There is no other way,
Just recycle it.
Save our planet,
Don't just bin it!

Charlotte Balston (14)
Ferndown Upper School, Ferndown

Remember

When I am gone, which could be tomorrow,
Will you remember me with laughter or sorrow?
Will you cry at my memories,
Or smile at how I used to be?

When I am buried 6-ft under,
Remember that I loved the thunder.
But do not cry as you hear the boom,
Talk to me, I'll be in the room.

When life for me abruptly ends,
Remember that we'll still be friends
Remember that I loved the sea,
If there's a beach in Heaven, that's where I'll be!

So when I am gone, which could be tomorrow,
Will you remember me with laughter or sorrow?

Harriet Whiting (15)
Ferndown Upper School, Ferndown

Special Day

The second biggest day of her life.
Here it is
Should it be silk, short or long?
Straps or none?
But she knows
She's been dreaming of it.
Each day it gets clearer and clearer -
The silk underlay
White as snow.
The netting skirt overlay
Enhanced with sparkles,
Glittering with sequins.
It's her angel dress.
He'll love it
Watching it glide down the aisle
On their special day.

Melissa Ingleton (14)
Ferndown Upper School, Ferndown

Battery Child

I'm a typical battery child,
So is everyone I know.
We've lost our identification,
Our hearts are filled with woe.

Each morning the old farmer wakes us up,
With loud squawking and complaining sounds.
We are let out of our hard 5-foot by 3-foot cages,
And our feathers are sown on, neatened up and brushed
into position.
Each one of us is fed one bowl of muesli or toast,
Then we have a brush injected into our mouths and wiggled around.
Next the feathers on our back are stuffed with books and pens,
After which we are bundled into large carrying cases
with four wheels on.
A noise starts up, the case moves quickly and many loud clucks
are heard.
At the end of the journey, other farmers unload us, opening the doors
of our cage.
We have to quickly fly into a new set of cages,
Where we will have to learn stuff like the 2 times tables and how to flap
our wings.
However a nice break comes halfway through the cruel
torture method,
When our relieved feather-covered souls are released from
our cages.
Each of us flies once around the social area, then is returned.
It is very quiet - the farmers demand silence as they are very strict.
Therefore at 30 clucks after 15 long clucks, we are happy.
This is because we are let back onto the large things with wheels,
And transported back home for one bowl of cornflakes.
At 19 long clucks after at least 3 hours in a battery cage, the lights
are put out.
We fall asleep ready for another torture tomorrow.

Why can't we just live naturally?

Kasey Watson (12)
Guernsey Grammar School, St Andrews

Wasted Breath

Don't waste your breath on a bitter word
That no one wishes to have heard,
Or on mutterings of a better past,
Remember it, things change, so nothing'll last.

Don't waste your breath on constant regret,
Take better action and then forget,
Or only voicing intentions, meaning well
For they say these pave the road to Hell.

Don't waste your breath on another lie
For it's the truth that is rated high,
Or on empty promises that you can't keep
As wasted words are those you repeat.

Don't waste your breath arguing with peers
Your words will be falling on deaf ears,
Or with your teachers, disagreeing
For you stand to fight for nothing.

Don't waste your breath on another apology,
Think before you speak instead of being sorry,
And this to others you could teach
Only when you practise what you preach.

Katie Fallaize (17)
Guernsey Grammar School, St Andrews

My Generation

Loud new music beats,
New fashion and shoes on feet.

Mobiles, laptops, iPods and MP3s,
Overspending, lots of parties.

Celebrity stories and news headlines,
Size zero and stupid crimes.

Late-night programmes on television
Homework with exam revision.

Designer clothes and hair,
Racism and human scares.

Memories embed your brain,
Can't forget the weird and insane.

Holidays in rain or sun,
Friends, family and lots of fun.

Fill your life with every sensation,
Because, this is my generation.

Chloe Norman (13)
Guernsey Grammar School, St Andrews

Friends

As we walk, side by side,
She tells me her story, I tell her mine,
As we talk, we laugh and smile,
She tells me jokes, both funny and vile,
As we whisper, mouth to ear,
She tells me things, only for me to hear,
As we share secrets, hand on heart,
She tells me how she couldn't bear for us to part,
I believe that we'll be friends forever,
Ones who are there, when and wherever.

Emilia Still (12)
Guernsey Grammar School, St Andrews

My Generation

Motorola, Nokia, Samsung,
All of these words mean the same thing -
Phone.

Mac, Vista, Microsoft,
All of these words mean the same thing -
Computer.

iPod, CD, mp3,
All of these words mean the same thing -
Music.

Superb, fantastic, brilliant.
All of these words mean the same thing -
My generation!

Nathan Hazzan (12)
Guernsey Grammar School, St Andrews

The World Was Once Wrapped
In A Golden Blanket

The human race, so inferior and small,
The footstep we leave, so superior it seems to all.
The trees that fall, people are there but do they hear?
The icecaps that melt, is humanity not the one to sink?
Monkeys play in hollowed-out homes,
While polar bears once flourished, in now disappearing floes.
Dolphins glide through oil-slicked blue,
Whilst unheard birds whistle their wise tune:
The Earth was once wrapped in a golden blanket,
Where species lay undisturbed and peaceful,
Then generations came and we built and we bred,
Without once looking over the path we did tread.

Clarice Parrott (12)
Guernsey Grammar School, St Andrews

My Generation Poem

'So, what's on your mind today, son?'
God, if he only knew . . .
About the girl next door whom I like.
About the fact that I'm growing up
and things are happening to my body
that they told me would happen.
About the worries that I seem to be getting a bit too thin.
About the old phone I have whereas everyone else has these
ultra modern phones that shoot lasers or something.
About the constant fear that my uncle will die in that pointless
war in Iraq.
About my hair which hasn't been cut in two years
and so everyone calls, 'Get a haircut!'
About my mum and dad who keep shouting at each other . . .

'Nothing, Dad,' I replied,
I didn't want to trouble him.

David Campbell   (12)
Guernsey Grammar School, St Andrews

My Generation

I'm walking through town,
All the cliques hanging round,
The ongoing war,
Between chavs, emos and more,
Yobs causing trouble,
Schoolgirls spending double,
All the young couples out for lunch,
Some lazy people eating brunch,
Lots of different fashion sense,
Poor beggars collecting pence,
People out walking pets,
People thinking opposites,
Mags full of anorexic models,
Education Board says we're eating double,
While we're on our mobile phones,
Our parents are home sorting loans,
The adult world is so different from ours,
Repaying debt and driving cars,
I hope our generation never dies out,
Because if it does, I'll *scream* and *shout!*

Jessica Savident (12)
Guernsey Grammar School, St Andrews

My Generation

Five fruit and vegetables,
Not too much sugar,
Organic vegetables,
Know your GDAs.

In the 'olden days',
I wonder,
Would you know your GDAs?
Something to ponder.

Need more exercise,
An hour every day,
Stop size zero models,
Eat up your food today.

In the 'olden days',
I wonder,
How skinny were you?
Something to ponder.

Hole getting bigger,
Locally sourced food,
Air miles, exhaust fumes,
I'm so confused!

Think back to your childhood,
No war, no politics, no Saddam Hussain,
It was better in your day,
So don't complain.

Heather Ewert (12)
Guernsey Grammar School, St Andrews

Talking 'Bout My Generation

So what if I'm different?
I'm not like you

I don't wear make-up
Or eyeshadow too

I'm young, I'm free
And I do what I want

I don't go out Fridays
Don't go and get drunk

I'm not like the others
Who copy and leech

I'm an individual; I do as I please

I don't smoke cigarettes -
Think they smell bad

I do get my work done
It makes my mum glad

I like my life
I do it my way

And if you can't accept that
I've got no more to say.

Ellie Perchard (15)
Hautlieu School, Jersey

Look Deeper

In times gone by, childhood was free
Now worries engulf our minds.
I watch the pictures
On the TV screen
A never-ending conveyor belt
A record of our wrongs.
I see the burning cities,
Smoking guns and children's tears,
And I wish that it was just
A dream.
They say we are
Lazy
Uncaring
Selfish
But it is not so
For I hear the tap-tap of machine guns
And I hear the screams of pain
But I feel so small, so worthless;
A bright star lonely in the universe.
I want to make a difference, change the world
But I know it's just a vision
That I can't create alone.
Everyone must unite;
Love
Help
Care for their fellows.
We are not all insensitive, antisocial.
Look deeper and it becomes clear;
We're all the same inside
You just have to search hard enough.

Sarah Gouyette (15)
Hautlieu School, Jersey

My Appearance

Never in my life,
Did I hurt someone with a knife.

Lots of people now carry a gun,
I never did that under the sun.

People think that I am really rough,
But inside I am not so tough.

On the street people fear me, most of the time,
But when did I ever commit a crime?

That's where I'm at,
This ain't no act.

Just take ten minutes to talk to me,
Then all you people will really see.

'What a nice young man'
Just stuck in life's jam.

On their faces people get a big surprise,
Because of my extraordinary size.

Generally I am kind,
The kind of person people don't seem to mind.

So why, because of my appearance,
Do people want me to make a disappearance?

Breffni Potter (15)
Holyport Manor School, Holyport

Being Ignored

No one likes being ignored
When they've done something good
Just like if they've done a good piece of work
Or
Even when they've built something
Or
Just had a good time
Even if they've helped someone
And I like it when it's noticed
That *I* did it
Or
Just done something for someone
Even if it's their work
Or
Just with something else.

Richard Creffield (15)
Holyport Manor School, Holyport

Football

I like football
It is good fun to play
I get tired when I'm playing football outside
We always wear the same clothes
When we play a game outside
In class we get water in a mug
We all have to go to the showers
They are cold and everyone runs out of them
I love it.

Robert Barker (14)
Holyport Manor School, Holyport

The Boy On Holiday

Holidays
Should be happy
Seeing the boy made me unhappy
He was very young
His mum and dad were evil
They punched their son
He cried
Everyone looked
They were angry
A person complained
It did not do any good
He was still punched
I still think of him.

Jamie Hepburn (13)
Holyport Manor School, Holyport

Ben's Rap

Now everybody in the hall today
Put your hands in the air and clap away
James Blunt has sung and made you sad
I'm here now to make you glad
My name is Ben and I'm here to win
So pin back your ears and I'll begin
Jingle them bells and cook them pies
The man in the red suit is riding the skies
So all you kids had better be swell
Or Simon Cowell will be ringin' your bell!'

Ben Shepherdly (15)
Holyport Manor School, Holyport

Evey

I met a girl named Evey at my youth club.
She has beautiful blonde hair and is exactly my age.
A few weeks later I am still in love with Evey
But I feel so scared to tell her.
I don't even have the heart to tell my brother.
I met a girl named Evey at my youth club.

Evey can be quiet or witty,
But I feel a little bit frightened of telling her so.
I'm writing this story as a little pretty ditty!

I met a girl named Evey at my youth club!

Adam James Potter (14)
Holyport Manor School, Holyport

My Lovely Teacher

She helped me in the bad times
When I needed help she was there
She listened when I wanted to talk
When I was happy she was kind
If I was ill, she would look after me.

Who is she?
My teacher, Miss Cole.

David Harber (13)
Holyport Manor School, Holyport

Proms

Riding in the limousine,
Long, white and shiny.
Sparkling lights, floating balloons,
Food and drink on the tables.
Music playing.
I sing the songs,
We are all dancing like a pop party.
Guys in suits, girls in dresses,
Make-up, jewellery,
Prom kings and queens.
How exciting!

Sabina Nilsson (15)
Holyport Manor School, Holyport

BFF
Best Friends Forever

Friends are cool
Friends are fun to have
We always laugh, we always talk
We always stick together
I go to friends for advice
You can always trust them with problems
You can always talk together
Sometimes we have good times
But remember, we always remain friends.

Gagandeep Juttla (15)
Holyport Manor School, Holyport

Music And TV

Music is a famous thing in the 21st century
Lots of people dance to music
People also go to discos and clubs to enjoy the sound of music
TV
TVs are a portable form of entertainment
They are a fantastic invention
People can watch programmes and films on them
TVs can be carried around.

Jamie Lloyd (16)
Holyport Manor School, Holyport

Fireworks

I like fireworks
I like the noise
I like the beautiful colours
They make me feel happy
I like to watch them
With my mum, dad and sister Natalie.

Sam Peacock (15)
Holyport Manor School, Holyport

Teachers

Teachers here, teachers there,
There are teachers everywhere!

Don't do this and don't do that,
Sit up straight and please don't shout!

Teachers here, teachers there,
There are teachers everywhere!

Study hard to pass your test
Follow the rules and do your best.

Teachers here, teachers there,
There are teachers everywhere!

Aimee Boissiere (11)
Le Rocquier School, St Clement

Cars

Brrrrm, and they're off, change the gear.
Put your foot down.
Listen to the engine flowing.
Crowd cheering you on.
Overtake rockers.
You're in the lead
And across the line.
Lift the shining trophy.
Get a medal and flowers.

Daniel Heaven (11)
Le Rocquier School, St Clement

With Or Without

With you, I realised my dreams,
Without you I'm stuck in limbo.
With you, you gave me my sanity,
Without you, I'm driven over the line.

This pain of being alone is just too real.

With you, the time never seemed to matter,
Without you, life just passes me by.
With you, I was always late to everything,
Without you, I've been early ever since.

Some things, time cannot erase.

With you, I swept away all of your tears,
Without you, I let my crying overcome me.
With you, I held your hand through good and bad,
Without you, I wander through my overgrown terror.

It's too late now, signed with stamp and seal.

With you, I slept knowing you were safe.
Without you, I lie awake worrying for myself.
With you, you opened my eyes to our future.
Without you, I close my eyes and wait for it all to go.

I await through the cold for the one last embrace.

Standing here alone with my mind, I do nothing but wonder,
And slowly feel myself, slipping, falling and going under.

Stefan Le Marquand (15)
Le Rocquier School, St Clement

The Environment Is Changing

The environment is falling,
Curling at our feet,
If we don't do something about its calling,
Then it will roll to defeat.

Install solar panels,
Install wind turbines,
If we don't act fast the channel will be bigger.

Cold in the winter,
Don't use the heater,
Wrap up warm and no more cold winters,

Peels, skins and food waste,
Don't let go,
Compost them and that is the end of the waste,

When cutting trees.
Don't burn the land,
Let it grow back into trees,
Give nature a helping hand,

Cars, yeah, they may be fast,
But it's much better by bike,
And don't think you're last,

Storms, hurricanes, twisters and tidal waves,
If we don't help
We will be lost in our own caves,
Calling for our own help.

Raoul Crosby (12)
Le Rocquier School, St Clement

Our Form Teacher

Our form teacher's name is Mr Roberts.
He is really great.
We've only had him for seven weeks
And that's even better
(Than other teachers . . .)
Our form teacher's name is Mr Roberts.
He is really great,
The work he sets gets harder and harder
than it was in primary.
(But we're fine with it . . .)
Our form teacher's name is Mr Roberts.
He is really great,
He teaches LIA which is a mixture of lessons
like geography, history and other things.
(That's our form teacher)!

Danielle Le Verdier (11)
Le Rocquier School, St Clement

My Tennis Racket

My tennis racket is blue,
It has a green grip.
I love my strings because they are blue.
My tennis racket is the best, like me.
We work together and we work hard.
We can do everything as long as we're together.
my tennis racket is magic.
It makes me win everything.
Me and my racket travel everywhere.
We both like tennis.
We are the best.
I love my tennis racket.

Audrey Bois (12)
Le Rocquier School, St Clement

The World

The world is big
The world is blue
If we pollute the Earth
It will kill you!

The sea is blue
The skies are grey
Pollution will end
Your day.

Bombs falling on the ground
Trees dead, falling down
Children crying, very hard
At least we're safe and unharmed.

This is the place where I live
It's unsafe and a risk
But this is the place that I love
I wouldn't give it up for the world and above.

Charlotte Turner (11)
Le Rocquier School, St Clement

War On Iraq

War can be bad, loads of lives lost,
Although this war is illegal.
Rest is what the world needs.

Or peace worldwide.
Not war, as that is bad.

In this world where we live
Rest and peace are what we need
And a worldwide community.
Quietness and love.

Matthew Martin (14)
Le Rocquier School, St Clement

Twin Towers 9/11

T umbles down
W ith people
I nside
N ot looking.

T rying to get
O ut
W hen people are
E verywhere
R unning and
S houting.

T hen people
W atching what's happening
I n shock
N ot knowing what made this happen.

T errorists killing people
O rdinary lives wrecked
W hen people are sad
E veryone cries
R unning, getting help and in shock
S adly people die.

Catherine Richards (13)
Le Rocquier School, St Clement

The Scary Spider

S cary and hairy
P uts flies in its web
I n and out of hiding places
D estroyed when I step on it
E ven though it's dead, it's still freaky
R evolves into a monster in your mind.

Connie Lopez-Rubio (14)
Le Rocquier School, St Clement

Poems

England got hammered by South Africa in the group,
But we scrapped through by beating Tonga and Samoa
When Wilkinson came back from injury then we played
                    really well against Australia and beat them.
England were going to play against tournament hosts France
Who had beaten tournament favourites New Zealand.
When we played France, Wilkinson won it for us
With a drop goal and conversion
We met South Africa who were a bit too strong for us.

Elvio Da Silva (13)
Le Rocquier School, St Clement

My Generation

They may glare at you in disgust,
Or speak to you with their tongue curled,
They're in the alleys, at the park,
But are they taking over the world?

They're in the chippy,
They're watching you,
They have all the lies in the book,
With gum they chew.

Oh yes, oh yes,
Back in their day,
Such bad things,
Would never get the 'OK'.

But now it's different,
It matters what you wear,
Or even how you speak,
You get processed in their stare.

Can you escape?
Maybe you could,
But maybe the truth is,
They are just misunderstood.

Yazmin Farasat (13)
Lytchett Minster School, Poole

My Generation

Walking the streets,
The different looks that you meet,
The judgemental glare of prejudice,
Who is this?

The branded name of hooligan,
They don't know what they've begun,
The sense that there is a shadowy presence,
In our admittance.

When in a gang they like to presume,
We are trouble starting to fume.
Shrieking and yelling, swearing, breaking,
Causing havoc and trouble-making.

It is not fair to give us a name,
We are not all the same.
The looks of apparent disgust,
Don't necessarily fit all of us.

Watching, constantly aware,
Waiting to see what damage we shall share.
Bitter lies seem to form in their eyes,
Unaware one, does not mean all.

One image has overclouded us all,
Over the ones that stand and the ones that fall.
A hating nation,
Judging my generation.

Emma Milner (14)
Lytchett Minster School, Poole

My Generation

The people in the street they stare,
At all the clothes the teenagers wear,
They do not like us, not one little bit,
All those old people who just sit and knit.

They hate it when we are in a crowd,
They hate it when we say things loud,
The people who go and smoke in the woods,
The people who live under the hoods.

Everyone wants to be the same,
No one wants to get the blame,
Being popular is all we want,
Every day we try to flaunt.

We all think we've got it,
We all think we're fit,
Some of us do drugs and want booze,
The rest of us just have lots of shoes!

We call some chavs and emos,
We call some pikes and some greebos,
But overall our generation's good,
I suppose we are just misunderstood.

Pippa Woods (13)
Lytchett Minster School, Poole

My Generation

We're all different people
And we want to shout it loud,
But we try and try to be the same,
To fit in with the crowd.

You might say we're trouble,
But we're just misunderstood,
We're kids and we wanna have fun,
Before we go to adulthood.

Try to see us for who we are
And not the label we carry,
There is more to us than meets the eye,
Think who you used to be!

Jade Knight (13)
Lytchett Minster School, Poole

Through The Eyes Of . . .

Light protecting passing ships,
Waves lashing far below on the rocks,
Lonely seabirds wheel and cry.

The lighthouse stands firm above the ocean,
Lonely sentinel against the sea,
Seagulls soar over, biting the wind,
They fly so freely, yet here I am held.

So here I must stay
Minding lamp, tending fuel,
For rocks do not waver
And this strong sea is cruel.

Thomas McCabe (12)
Mullion School, Helston

Through The Eyes Of A Blind Person

I see darkness,
I feel so cold.
Emptiness around me,
No one to hold.

The light of the moon,
On the side of my face.
Silence all around me,
I'm in a deserted place.

Nobody knows,
I even exist.
Nobody to love me,
I'll never be missed.

Is that footsteps,
Coming near?
A stranger in the darkness,
Who I fear.

The footsteps have stopped,
My life's fading away.
I feel so helpless,
It's a very dark day . . .

Charlotte Lawlor (12)
Mullion School, Helston

Through The Eyes Of . . .

An orphan girl,
A lonely child,
A forgotten secret,
A heart so mild.

A broken heart,
A shattered smile,
The dear little thing,
A lonely child.

For longing peace,
A deadened soul,
It's an endless ditch,
A pit, a hole.

Abandoned here,
Left there,
She's just a child,
Wanting life somewhere.

The bitterness end,
It's hard to tell,
As if I loved
And knew her well.

I can't believe,
What has become,
Of that girl,
That once had fun . . .

The end has come,
Her greatest fear,
It's time to say,
Goodbye my dear.

Lowenna Trimble (12)
Mullion School, Helston

A Broken Child

A broken child,
Innocent and nice,
Daddy has a bad day,
So she pays the price.

Just a child,
Longing for love,
Sent from Heaven,
Up above.

Day after day,
Heart and soul shatter,
Bottles it up,
Like nothing's the matter.

It's life as she knows it,
Battered and bruised,
That sweet little girl,
With nothing to lose.

Body and mind,
Hurting so bad,
She's wondering what,
Made Daddy so mad.

Then one day,
He went too far,
Killing the girl,
The classroom star.

Simone Hawkings (12)
Mullion School, Helston

Through The Eyes Of A Baby Elephant

I see birds flying scarce
I hear footsteps coming from behind
I see Mum lying on the floor
I hear purring.

I see trees blowing
I hear the crumpling of leaves
I see blood trickling through the cracks on the floor
I feel burning on my dry skin.

I feel cold
I feel helpless
I feel dehydrated
I feel scared.

I want Mum
Why isn't she moving?
Still and quiet
I don't understand.

I need someone
I need help
I need water
I need Mum.

I see movement
I see a dark shadow
I see a tiger
Can he help me?
My life flashes before my eyes!

Charlotte Roberts (12)
Mullion School, Helston

The Estate

I walk down the road, with broken glass and cans,
That's the 'artwork' that decorates this desolate land.

I'm only new here, and the downward spiral has got me,
The spiral is a gang, and from it I can never be free.

I'm forced to go out with a spray can in hand,
The police come around the corner,
Their screeching sirens sound like a scary band.

I try to warn my so-called friends; they are too busy drawing
on a wall,
The police are coming closer, and all they care about is an
illegal scrawl.

Now the police are here, there's nowhere to run,
I get arrested for something I haven't done.

The handcuffs are on and so I've been framed,
There's a gun in my pocket and to my heart it is aimed.

The gun isn't mine and my innocence I protest,
I try to explain this is a misunderstood mess.

I'm facing some punishment and this I know,
I'm dying inside, but my feelings cannot show.

I get a month in prison, I suppose I should feel lucky,
But I've got a criminal record and that's something that will
always be with me.

Back to the gang for me, or my life will be on the line,
I've seen too many things and I've paid someone else's time.

The estate, the disgusting estate, now that is my home,
Even though I'm in a big gang, I've never felt more alone.

I walk down the road with broken glass and cans,
That's the 'artwork' that decorates this desolate land.

Bethany Noble (13)
St Bernard's Convent School, Slough

Looking But Not Seeing

Every night I lie in sighs,
Thoughts spinning through my mind.
The only thoughts in my mind are of you,
Wonderful, faultless you.

When at school you see right through me,
I'm a loser, a freak, an idiot.
You see right through me,
When you do notice me, you look but do not see.

If I told you how I feel you'd run like a rabbit in the headlights,
When I see you, my heart beats a million miles an hour.
What wouldn't I give for a minute, just one magical minute with you,
I've never felt like this before,
But I'm invisible to you.

Fern Matthews (12)
St Osmund's CE Middle School, Dorchester

My Generation

I want to see hours of dedication
To this beautiful population,
Of lush green trees and roaming elephants
With their gleaming ivory.
This is what I wish to see
But this is just a dream.
Destruction is what I see,
Pollution is what I smell.
Is there any hope,
Can it be sorted?
50 years from now,
The devastation could be huge.

Robbie Ward & Will Youngs
St Osmund's CE Middle School, Dorchester

Split In Two

I sit on my bed,
With the scene in my head,
Worried about what I've done,
Whether it's me or Mum.

Shaking with fear,
I shed a tear,
When Dad walked out,
I let out a shout.

I walked around with a shadow of doubt,
Why? Oh why, Dad, did you shut me out?

It's just Mum and me now,
No shouting or rows,
But now I know why,
I used to cry,
Because I was split in two.

Ellie Schamroth (12)
St Osmund's CE Middle School, Dorchester

Addiction

Chemicals are flowing, slowly down my throat.
Lungs filling with deadly toxic smoke.
Crawling around as slow as a snail.
Decaying my body gradually.
I want one more, just one more.

Lighting and puffing.
Coughing and choking.
Craving for nicotine, do I need help?
My brain is addicted to these poisonous sticks.
I want one more, just one more.

Ben Killian & Steven Kelley (12)
St Osmund's CE Middle School, Dorchester

The Kids Of Africa

Scared and hungry,
Poor kids of Africa are
Fighting for their lives.
Do you say:
'No Mum, I don't want that chicken?'
Those kids,
The kids of Africa,
Would treasure all the food you reject.
Do you give time to raise some cash
For the helpless little girl that was on the verge of death?
I bet you're thinkin', I don't care,
But if you were her,
I bet you'd dare
To change your mind.
We all take money and want the latest gadgets,
They'd be grateful for just one pencil!
You take clean water without a second glance,
They walk for hours for dirty slime.
Just think.

Kathryn Flint (12)
St Osmund's CE Middle School, Dorchester

New Year Sales

From the old
Into the new,
Fashion came
And fashion grew.

Flarey, flattery, short and tight,
Worn in the day and in the night.
So colourful and bold,
From the streets where it's cold.
Flooding the shops with lots of clothes,
Searching through all the rows.

Five pounds, ten pounds, fifteen and more,
As they pay before the door.
Crowds and crowds of people stand,
As they wait whilst hearing the band.
People screaming, people shouting,
Maybe even a little pouting.
Finally now, the shops are open,
As they push and shove into the shop that they love.

Katie Andrew (12)
St Osmund's CE Middle School, Dorchester

Da Streetz Today

The elderly panic-stricken,
The children feel uncomfortable,
Always looking around, on edge.
Vandalism,
Innocent killings,
Do we really want a world like this?

'Come on, chicken! Just do it!'
Sweaty palms,
Butterflies,
Heart pounding.
Numb arms,
Forcing eyes,
Bang!
Gone.
Can't believe it,
What have I done?

What caused me to do it:
Peer pressure,
Destructive games,
Self esteem,
Self-fulfilment?
All of these things seem silly now,
But not then,
I can't turn back time though, can I?
But I really wish I could.

Emily Bate (12)
St Osmund's CE Middle School, Dorchester

What Broke You In Two?

I sleep with a cloud above my bed,
I weep with your picture in my head.
I have tried not to cry,
I have tried, but how I cry.

Walking down the street every day,
I'll see your face in the grey.
I feel guilty, I feel scared,
I should have cared.

Mum, please tell me
Dad, what about you?
Please tell me,
What broke you in two?

Please come back,
I fell in the trap.
Could you forgive me,
Yes or no?
I guess I'll never know.

Kathrine Thompson-Ward (12)
St Osmund's CE Middle School, Dorchester

Dark And Light

If the world was peaceful
and there were no wars,
people would not despair
and cry at all the blood and gore.
But would have freedom, hope and happiness,
the future to explore.

Hilary Hansford (11)
St Osmund's CE Middle School, Dorchester

What Genre Do I Like?

Next time you're looking for a book in the library,
Or when you're in the book shop on the street,
Just think, what genre do I like?

Do I like fairy tale books,
With wizards and witches,
Unicorns and fairies,
With dwarfs that run dairies?

Do I like adventure books,
With a giant quest,
To rescue a beautiful girl,
Or to hunt down a special pearl?

Do I like romantic books,
With hugs and kisses,
People falling in love,
Plus a beautiful white dove?

Do I like horror books,
With zombies and aliens,
A bump in the night,
That will pin me to my bed with fright?

So next time you're looking for a book,
Think! What genre do I like?

Tom Whiter (11)
St Osmund's CE Middle School, Dorchester

My Generation

Walking up the street
As time goes by
Behind every door
There's a secret and a lie.

Number 21, a girl lives here
Sad, angry, tattered and torn
Living all alone
With a baby unborn.

Number 22, a boy screams
In the night,
But nobody listens
They just turn off the light.

Number 23, twins play on a swing
Thinking everything's happy
They don't know everything.

Walking up the street
As time goes by
Behind every door
There's a secret and a lie.

Alice Dodd (12)
St Osmund's CE Middle School, Dorchester

Why Me?

At night the streets are silent,
with shadows that appear violent.
The blazing heat of the sun disappeared
as did the thoughts in my head, they cleared.
Figures unknown to me raced through my mind,
I felt frustrated; as if there was something I couldn't find.
At night the streets are empty,
except for this one man, he moved towards me.
His eyes glowed like the dying cool on the fire,
if you thought him gentle, you'd be a liar.
With a gun that gleamed in the moonlight
containing a bullet that kills in a two-man fight.
He's like a cat; stalking his prey,
he'll hunt them down, come the day.
His teeth have a shimmer
like the stars' exquisite glimmer.
The wind silently roars,
as the man's hands turn to claws.
Bruises, scratches, a broken arm,
there's no reason for this, I did no harm.
This is the result of not giving into pressure,
but surely a bullet in your body is an extreme measure.
There should not be a consequence for this,
or any years of your life you miss,
but the mystery still remains
why give me drugs? Please, someone explain.
I know I've been told why before,
but it was only ever the funny side I saw.

Ashleigh Purvey
St Osmund's CE Middle School, Dorchester

Drugs

Drugs, they're takin' the nation, it's a complication,
We gotta work around it, there's no question 'bout it.
Everyone's getting high, shootin' up in the sky,
We gotta stop before we get nicked by a cop,
We have to get away - that'll be the day,
No more speed, fight the need,
Chuck away the fag. It is bad,
Crack, cocaine and cannabis, it's time for you to give it a miss,
Pot, weed and magic mushrooms too,
No one can give it up for ya - only you.
You think you can cope so ya keep takin' the dope,
But you'll lose control of ya dirty soul,
Your life's crashin' around ya: the dealers have found ya,
They want their money, they don't think it's funny,
They leave ya bleedin' and you start weepin',
They're laughin' in ya face, callin' you a disgrace,
I tried to warn ya, now death's round ya corner, drugs.

Luke Doherty (13)
St Osmund's CE Middle School, Dorchester

The Sonnet Of Helms Deep

I'm telling you of a battle long ago,
with elves, dwarves, men and a world of good and bad.
The battle of Helms Deep was in full flow,
where lives were lost for a prize to be had.
For the prize was a ring, a ring of great powers,
A ring to decide the fate of all things.
Desired by Saruman who controlled the two towers,
and held by a Hobbit named Frodo Baggins.
The battle was bloody, the battle was long,
the archers were fighting, arrows strung to their bows.
But the Orcs came in thousands, their might was too strong,
till out of the sunlight, great warriors arose.
The tables were turned - the Orcs were defeated,
but will this battle be repeated?

James Ashington (12)
St Osmund's CE Middle School, Dorchester

Discrimination

'Curlies are crazy'
'Blonds got no brain'
These words I am hearing
Everywhere, every day
While guns are firing
Out in Iraq
There are thugs conspiring
A cruel plan to attack
Forget about wars
We got battles at break
The victims try to ignore . . . but
How much more can they take?

Ginger hair means nothin'
It's what's inside that counts
Which is why this needs stoppin'
Before it gets out of bounds
Who cares how our hair is?
Who cares what we see?
The question is where's the justice
And where's the harmony?

Joe Rutter (12)
St Osmund's CE Middle School, Dorchester

Friends Forever

AF ter all we've been through,
 R emember those days?
 I thought I was your friend,
 E ven though I knew I was always sharing you.
 N ow I know the truth, I was never part of the picture,
 D emoted to a spare part, unloved and unwanted.
 S omehow your tricked me,
 H ooked me with your 'friends forever'.
 I 'm on my own now, even though I always was,
 P ersuaded me to stick with you, said we were soulmates,
 S o tell me now, why am I all alone?

Kerry Gorham (12)
St Osmund's CE Middle School, Dorchester

Iraq

Iraq, Iraq, Iraq,
The endless warfare goes on and on,
Iraq, Iraq, Iraq,
When will we leave and move on?
Iraq, Iraq, Iraq,
Innocent people fleeing the nation,
Iraq, Iraq, Iraq,
What are we fighting for?

Breaking news, breaking news,
Thousandth soldier died in Baghdad,
Breaking news, breaking news,
Suicide bomber causes terror in village,
Breaking news, breaking news,
US send in more troops,
Breaking news, breaking news,
The war shows no signs of ending soon.

Kieran Smith (12)
St Osmund's CE Middle School, Dorchester

Death

Feel the blood trickling down your cheek
Burns covering your face like a suffocating blanket
The feel as though you are dropping from immense height.

Hearing the crack of your bones
Your last sight a bullet looking you in the eye.

Death is not just game over, death is your last move,
Your last sight, the last sound, before your eternal rest.

Freezing at the sight with sadness in your eyes,
As another soul is carried away in the wind.

Max Warren (12)
St Osmund's CE Middle School, Dorchester

The Torture Of Bullying

Looking down on the girl with style,
Criticised for the clothes she wears.
Not knowing the fragile person,
Behind the mask of taunting fear.

The darkened truth covered up with a smile -
The marks on her body hidden away.
Feeling alone and vulnerable;
She wishes for the end of the torturous day.

Disappearing into the shadows of another,
It's like playing hide-and-seek.
Once the bullies find you, it's as if there's no escape.
The bullying getting inside her; ripping at what is left.
With no place to hide, she even wishes she was dead.
Staring eyes fixed on her,
Watching her every move.

Feeling alone and isolated, wondering what went wrong.
Starting off as such a small thing, inside she's left cold.

Becky Walsh (12)
St Osmund's CE Middle School, Dorchester

Earth Song Poem

The Earth a burning Hell filled with war and rain
Revolution, pollution, devastation and extinction
Catastrophe, fiasco, tragedy and pain
But I have a dream of a reborn Earth filled with love and joy
Shouting and singing of a girl and a boy
Rebuilding hopes and great leaders of the Earth
Rainbows, sunlight and the miracle of birth.

Pascal Chukwudozie Anyanjo (12)
St Osmund's CE Middle School, Dorchester

Laramie

You open your pack of laramie,
Smoking is killing your family,
Nobody likes you anymore,
Your girlfriend kicks you out the door.

You're wasting your money on the tar,
Then you get drunk at the bar,
With 4000 chemicals in them,
Smoking gives you black phlegm.

As for your lungs, they'll be black,
And your heart, same as that,
If you smoke you are mad,
Smoking is really, really bad.

But there are some ways to get rid of this,
Nicorette gum, give your girlfriend a kiss,
And then save your family,
From the chemical gas there can be.

Jack Merriott (12)
St Osmund's CE Middle School, Dorchester

The Earth Poem

People all around me are crying.
They do not realise how many people are dying.
This world that I live in is under destruction.
No human on Earth could start reconstruction.
Let's hope this world turns a bend.
Too late - It's already at the end.

Ollie Sohawon (12)
St Osmund's CE Middle School, Dorchester

Darkness

Imagine what it's like - darkness all around.
And some of those who are actually blind can't even hear a sound.

Diseases play a small part in this, this terrible thing called blindness.
There is so much help these days, filled with love and kindness.

It helps quite a lot, this help they receive.
They may struggle to learn; their blindness may never leave.

Some may have received it on the day they entered the world.
Others may have had accidents or darkness steadily unfurled.

Stevie Wonder is one of the many famous that are blind.
He has brought inspirational music to mankind.

You may never realise what blindness feels like inside.
But those who do come out about it are right not to hide.

We should look up to those courageous and strong.
Seeing nothing but darkness their whole life long.

Jasmine Cottrell (11)
St Osmund's CE Middle School, Dorchester

The Earth Poem

I don't know why, destruction is everywhere.
Wherever I look people dying and crying, it's just not fair,
Why, destruction everywhere.
The animals are going one by one, going extinct.
Dying in the sun.
No love is shown, they are not won.

But at least I can sleep in my comfortable bed, not dying in the sun.
I can eat and I can drink, I have a dad and a mum,
Always saying, 'What's up Bun?'
I'm just lucky but it is just unfair.
It's just not fair.

Freddie Stacey (12)
St Osmund's CE Middle School, Dorchester

60s, 70s And 80s

60s, 70s and 80s were the heydays,
Drugs, protests and Blondie were all the rage.
Free love was cool and Michael was black,
They had style, which we now lack.

Computers a myth; TVs brand new,
Hippies protesting at the zoo.
England were world champs,
Everyone had a lava lamp.

Cops were loaded with gear,
There were piercings in everyone's ears.
Disco fever every night,
With children playing with a groovy kite.

Madonna was new to pop,
While Wham were at the top.
My mum was in her teens,
Considered to be a beauty queen.

Yeah that was the time,
That I pay tribute to with this rhyme.
Now it's all in the past,
The impression it leaves will forever last.

Lauren Coffey (12)
St Osmund's CE Middle School, Dorchester

The Killings Of Another Day

Frolicking around the field, their cotton bud tails swing to and fro,
The morning dew soaks through the grass
The sun radiates its burning glow.
A small white face of glistening fear
An icy sound of a sparkling tear.
The shadows cast their soundless loom,
The sun falls hastily from the darkened sky
As truck doors shout their deafening *boom!*
They leave their past behind . . .

The slaughterhouse their place of rest -
RIP to their cowardly experiences.
Walking through the carcasses,
Their brains blank out this final test.

Their memories lost forever,
Their bodies chucked away,
For the people there that killed them
It's just another working day.

Is this the future that we need?
To pollute our bodies, to fill our greed!
Their helpless lives are shot away,
The killings of another day . . .

Chloe Jefferies (12)
St Osmund's CE Middle School, Dorchester

Why Can't I Be Invisible?

I wear a label around my neck.
It's tattooed on my forehead and
It's all I think about.
I'm walking down the corridor,
And everyone's staring at me
I know they're all thinking the same;
The world whizzes round my mind.
They stop in their stride and glare
At me with piercing eyes.

The sound of the bell makes my spine tingle with fear.
I try to camouflage myself in a bunch of people
But they spot me already,
There is nowhere to run and nowhere to hide.
They're marching towards me like an army ready for battle,
Everyone goes soundless, observing me like hawks.

Then it's the beating,
Then it's the insults, they're flying at me like little birds
Then they get louder and louder
And then they start ripping me up inside.
Finally it stops, they've left me in peace,
But what's in store for me tomorrow?

Emily Diaz & Laura Caines (12)
St Osmund's CE Middle School, Dorchester

Bullies

All alone. Why can't anyone help me?
I'm not fat, I'm not ugly,
I'm not unloved, I'm not skinny,
I need to escape from this name-calling hell-hole.
Look in the mirror, what do I see?
Oh my God, is this really me?

Chavs and pikeys,
Emos and goths,
No need for the labels,
this is just me,
I dress how I like
I do what I want,
Don't judge a book by its cover,
Read it before you miss it.

I need to get this,
I need to get that,
Just so I can be like everyone else.
All the latest crazes, starting up a blaze.

Name-callers and bullies,
Backstabbing friends,
they hang with you and have some fun,
Next thing you know,
They push you to the ground.

Why do they do it?
Where is the fun?
What do they accomplish?
When will they stop?

Poppy Cranswick & Rebecca Diaz (12)
St Osmund's CE Middle School, Dorchester

The Depressing Life Of A Teenager

My life is turning upside down,
peer pressure making me drown.
Deep in the crowd I swallow and shake,
every day I worry about break.
Friends forcin' me to smoke,
drugs bein' forced down my throat.
Drinkin' stuff I shouldn't drink,
parties full of people who reek and stink.
People in and out of rooms,
doin' stuff adults do.
Plannin' lives we are not gonna live,
if we carry on like this.

Parents' expectations rising,
just cos bruv's got revising.
Why should I be like them,
walkin' into the Dragon's Den?

Lookin' up at the sky,
why in a few years' time
most of that may be gone.
Air pollution going on and on.

Flirtin' with boys I don't even like,
just let me go and ride my bike.
Paedophiles sittin', waitin',
children on the Internet taken.
Not knowing what will happen.

Violence at my home
makes bruv and sis moan.
My body is not a book you can judge,
so why do you bear a grudge?
What life is this I'm livin'
in this body I'm given?

Juliette Bone (12)
St Osmund's CE Middle School, Dorchester

Modern Day

'That's you,' Mum said,
as I climbed out of bed,
watching her friendly scowl,
going green, being mean,
with the wars, poverty,
what happened to all the peace?

'It's your fault, what happened to this world,' Mum states,
but I want to sort it out!
Her cigarettes, rusty car,
in the rain, through the pain,
here comes the back of her hand.

Like crocodiles,
she thinks we're wild,
and the pressure's too much for me,
the others use drugs, but I'm not a thug,
so I'll find out where she hides her gun,
they take it out on me,
kicking off in full knowledge that I'm near,
tale-telling till the teacher tuts,
found her weapon now,
how does it work?
Doesn't matter, the end result will be the same,
not loaded, what a shame,
but wait - it doesn't need to be!
I'll still stand strong,
I will be free,
I'm not wrong; it's not me,
I'll fight for it; I'll build an army,
holding my protest higher,
here comes the peaceful war . . .

Amy Bradford (12)
St Osmund's CE Middle School, Dorchester

My Childhood

I love my childhood.
It's great to mess about with a friend,
It's fun to go around the bend.
It's brill to play with all my mates,
To go out with boys, as really cute dates.
I also love my toys and games,
Having lots of laughs, and lots of shames.
It's wicked to have fun at the park,
At school I love getting an excellent mark.
Sport is fun too, synchro is fab,
And as for make-up, I love having a dab.
The TV and its channels rule,
The computer and the Internet; cool!
I like listening to my music all day,
And to go to sleepovers and play.
There is plenty of other things too,
I can think of more, can you?

But some things I know aren't as great,
Like falling out with a special mate.
I hate the dentists and injections,
Although they're good and get rid of infections.
Going to bed early isn't the best,
And as for chores, just give me a rest!
But sometimes when I point this out,
I get grounded and put on a pout.
There is quite a few more, but they aren't as bad,
I still don't like them but they don't make me as mad.

In just a few years I will be a teen,
But I'll try not to be really stressy and mean.
I really don't want to grow up; never,
But now I know,
My childhood won't last forever!

Jessica Element (11)
St Osmund's CE Middle School, Dorchester

Talkin' 'Bout My Generation

The gangsters of today are hangin' all over the place
With their slang like 'Gimme your money or I'll bust you in ya face'.

It's all 'bout partying and getting high
Makin' someone bleed and giving smokin' a try.

Kids doing stuff they see on TV
Playin' with guns like on Die Hard 3.

I got a criminal record list
It goes on for miles
Got locked up for quite a while.

I like to stay out and get drunk and wasted
My rep's so bad to the old people I'm globally wasted.

Public enemy No. 1, that's me
I'll break in ya house and steal ya plasma TV.

I hijacked a Porsche just yesterday
You should have seen the owner's face as I drove away.

Damn you cops, all tryin' to catch me
NYC finest, ain't got nothin' on me!
Holla!

Matthew Hurley (12)
St Osmund's CE Middle School, Dorchester

Weeks, Months And Years

My weeks are busy but are they too much?
I start on Monday with samba, singing and dance.
On Tuesday I toot and honk on my clarinet.
Wednesday I work on music theory.
On Thursday I join in the centenary of scouting at guides.
Next, on Friday, I dance and skip at cheerleading.
Weekends I play keyboard and on Sunday I swim.

My nana didn't do half as many things; but what did she do?
She played with dolls and experimented with chemistry.
She had ballet and tap lessons but there were no clubs.

In the future my children's children may do even less.
What about new-found technology?
Will they just sit and press buttons?
Will they forget how to sing and swim
Or would there be no world left to live in?
100 years in the future our Earth could be water!
What do we do?

Weeks, months and years until I die,
But I'm going to make the best of it!

Annabel Macklin (11)
St Osmund's CE Middle School, Dorchester

Pet Poem

Animals can comfort you,
even when you're worried.
They can certainly look after you
and get you through such misery.

If you need a friend to talk to,
or just a friendly hug,
they're just the ones you need to go to,
not a teenage thug.

If you've lost your family,
pets can help there too!
They bring back all the happy times,
not the sad, sad news.

If you have some reading trouble,
turn straight toward your pet!
Read aloud for them to hear,
you'll soon find that you're set.

Pets also need to be looked after,
brushed and fed all of the time!
After that they're there again,
always there to be a friend!

Carina Clark (12)
St Osmund's CE Middle School, Dorchester

Smoking

Lighting up the killer,
Setting its end alight,
The little addictive damager,
Runs into your life.
Sucking out the suicide mixture,
Putting life in threat,
My life now revolves around that fixture
And everyone I have met.
Breathing out the bully of a gas,
The sky now looks like overcast,
Rotten teeth and yellow nails,
Everything I possess has horrific smells.
My arteries clogged up like plugs,
Everyone refuses affectionate hugs,
My lungs are a black rattly cage,
No one wants to give me a wage.
Life could end tomorrow or the next,
One little thing can make huge effects.

Georgia Viller (12)
St Osmund's CE Middle School, Dorchester

The Killin' Crew

Pull the trigger!
Go on. Go on.
No! No! No!

Raging, bitter, resentful; that's the streets today.
Hide! Take cover! Shout for help!
The killin' crew's out to play.

Pull the trigger!
Go on. Go on.
No! No! No!

Propelling bullets in the head.
Dagger and they're gone.
Disguise, retreat, hide away.
Run! Run! Run!

Pull the trigger!
Go on. Go on.
Bang, bang!
Gone.

Helen Carter (12)
St Osmund's CE Middle School, Dorchester

My Poem

Pollution builds in the air
Driving cars everywhere
No light
No strength
The Earth just sits there
But there is power
There is strength
The human power
We *can* stop the fighting
War and pollution
Together *we can* stop, achieve anything!

Jahlemn David (12)
St Osmund's CE Middle School, Dorchester

Our Generation

Trees swaying in the wind,
Loud shouting from within our generation
Animals screeching as the claws sink in.
Our generation
A cry of laughter, shower of pain.
Our generation
Cars polluting, sirens ringing.
Our generation
Tornadoes twisting,
Hurricanes blowing.
Our generation
Deep in the darkness, out in the light
We're killing the world
Now put up a fight.
Our generation.

Evan Cumber (12)
St Osmund's CE Middle School, Dorchester

Earth Poem

I wish when I wake,
The sky is blue,
Like a giant lake.
I wish when I wake,
The grass is green with ragged tips,
But as comfortable as a fluffy rug.
But when I dream I wish I could imagine,
Myself flying as high as the clouds,
Just sitting watching time go by,
But in my dreams,
All I can imagine is torturing souls,
With pain-filled deaths
But could all be stopped in a simple minor breath.

Connor Gould (12)
St Osmund's CE Middle School, Dorchester

The World

The world is a fragile china cup,
Threatening to break at any point.
Global warming heating it to extremes.
Rubbish filling it up to the brim,
Slowly gaining cracks.

Slowly and surely the world is gaining cracks,
Lots of pollution,
Rainforest reduction,
That is the story of the world.

If the china cup breaks,
The mountains collapse,
The sea floods,
The land sinks.
Nothing left.

Matthew Hart (12)
St Osmund's CE Middle School, Dorchester

Our Dead World

Death, darkness and black,
Millions of people killed at heart,
Slicing hearts lead to stabbing pain,
People think that is all our fault,
We have all this loss,
But
Growing cheerfulness fading our pains,
Will make this world spin again,
Waking with no fear of war,
This shouldn't happen anymore,
What have we done?

Ellie Clark (12)
St Osmund's CE Middle School, Dorchester

Really More Of A Song

Music phones a-blarin'
to strangers we be larin'!
We're the thugs on the street,
living life to a beat.

Sitting in a classroom,
pouring over math tomes.
We're not really that bad,
the way you treat us is sad.

Banning hoodies and caps,
you think our minds are in lapse.
We're the future of your nation,
I'm talkin' 'bout my generation.

Louise Williamson (15)
Sandhurst School, Sandhurst

My Genes!

I come from a gene.
Not from the type you wear,
The type that is in your body.
I think I was made from my mum or dad's ancestors,
Uncles, aunties, Dad's family.
No one really knows.

But I definitely know I inherited some of my dad's genes,
That's how I became a boy
And I definitely know that I inherited some of my mum's genes
Because of my moods!

But the main things you see, what makes me,
Are my genes!

Sam Alford (12)
Shaftesbury School & Sports College, Shaftesbury

Nineties (90s) Kid

(Talkin' 'Bout My Generation)

I was born in the 90s,
And I lived for TV.
The shows in the morning
Were something to see.

The Spice Girls were boring,
But Aqua were cool.
Pop had arrived
And it definitely ruled.

I had Furbees and yo-yos,
Pogs and Beanies.
There were scooters and Rubix
As seen on TV.

I loved Goosebumps and Game Boys,
I thought Spyro was a legend.
I played Tekken and Zelda,
Oh, I really was in Heaven.

But now it's all gone,
And nobody remembers.

Now it's iPods and Blu-ray,
Terror and war,
Death after death,
Oh, jeez, please no more.
I remember the 90s,
And I wish I was there,
When the troubles I had
Were so simple and rare.

Lianne Hooper (17)
Shaftesbury School & Sports College, Shaftesbury

Generation Doom

Some sort of journey
Some sort of light
Overwhelming darkness
An everlasting plight

The sorrow and greed
The hatred inside
The fight for our needs
With nature defiant

Overhanging shadows
Forever stricken death
Everything that haunts us
Is stuck in our heads

We feel the pain of life
The lure of death
From the rising might
Of oppression ahead

With no love, no life
No reason to live
With all that we've seen
And all we did

To leave for a world
That we just don't know
That we can never trust
For a hope we cannot hold
For a breath we cannot muster

So,
Will this world welcome me to madness?
Will that be madly in love?
Or will my mind be hissed to bitterness?
Will I be kissed or will I be shoved?

Matthew Crumpler (17)
Shaftesbury School & Sports College, Shaftesbury

Forever In Their Debt

Mary Jane, 84, draws her curtains to.
There, behind closed doors, she does as she needs to.
The village folk rarely see her at corner shop or mass.
For she threw it all away in a summer now long past.
There behind closed doors she gets herself a key
And lifts from the mantelpiece a chest that once held tea.
A turn, the click, a moment's pause -
She dries an eye and remembers its cause.
Gathering together she withdraws a few treasured things -
Thrice-worn medal, his sepia photo, a pair of officer's wings.
Some letters, a faded forget-me-not (as if she could forget!)
And a crumpled tear-stained telegram: 'The air ministry regret . . .'
The tears come again, but silent now, and proud.
For not all the love in the world has to be said aloud.
Turning from the fire grate she takes it to a chair -
Hands it to the girl who waits patiently there.
'I told you I would show you,' says a kind Mary Jane
'I first met him by the tree up old Longford Lane . . .'
And so Kate hears the story of her own Grandpa Fred,
Waves off his plane that night as she sleeps tucked up in bed.
For Kate is only six and has yet to learn the cost
Of what it was her grandmother's generation lost.
Yet Mary Jane smiles to see her sleep this way,
Thinks Fred would have been glad of what he bought
For the price he had to pay.

Just so long as Kate's fingers never type: 'Today's children forget . . .'

Robert Broughton (16)
Shaftesbury School & Sports College, Shaftesbury

My Generation

My generation is alright
We get into our average fight
Though we're not all that cool
We're just fools
And we stay up all day and night

We all listen to rock and rap
Even though it's a load of c**p
To most people old music is a fright
To me it's alright,
Now the music is so loud you can't even nap

We walk about holding knives
We like to threaten innocent lives
We skip school just for pleasure
And take drugs for our leisure
And wouldn't respect our wives

We wear our trousers so low
That our cheap pants show
We wear a baseball cap on our head
Way too much like my gran said
But do I listen? No

So will we still be like this when we're old
Or will we all be told?
I expect the next generation will be like this
I myself will give it a miss
Because I'm the next one to go bald!

Gareth Way (13)
Shaftesbury School & Sports College, Shaftesbury

Oldification

Why do oldies talk 'bout their generation
And tell it like some inspiration?
Then they make you listen like it's an obligation
And complain 'bout your concentration.

Then they start talking 'bout some railway station
It's meant to be your fascination
But it's only going to be your destination
If on trains you get a nice sensation

Then they start complaining 'bout today's education
And say it needs a transformation
If you do bad you're going to end up in a service station
And then you'll regret your lack of education

But they do stop once they have their medication
It's like some sort of relaxation
They could almost be in a state of meditation

So I flick on a TV station
And now in peace I can watch my animation.

Tim Hardiman (15)
Shaftesbury School & Sports College, Shaftesbury

Talking 'Bout My Generation

Looking in a mirror, what do I see?
A fat, ugly person with a thin person inside
Listening to music, what do I hear?
The words that are giving us a message
Hearing the news, what do I hear?
Wars, lies, competition and hate
I look around the streets and I see . . .
Happy people laughing and having fun
I walk across the school playground and I see . . .
Children hand in hand, messing around
As I walk down the empty road I feel . . .
All eyes on me although no one is around
I walk past a homeless person, he says . . .
'A penny for your thoughts but a dollar for your insides'
It made me think this is our generation.

Jodie Robinson (15)
Shaftesbury School & Sports College, Shaftesbury

Paranoia

Why you starin' at me?
Is it cos I is black
Or is it cos I is white?
Is it cos I ain't 15 an' I'm pregnant
Again
Or cos I'm a single dad in a council house?
Is it cos I'm a queer, a gay
Or is it cos I let my emotions show?
What is it?
Is it me you're starin' at
Or you?

You starin' at me cos I ain't normal?
Cos I ain't got no legs, or no arms, or no ears?
Is it cos I have a family
Or cos I don't
Or cos I never did?

You starin' at me cos I'm different
Or cos you aren't?

Tom Whitfield (17)
Shaftesbury School & Sports College, Shaftesbury

Will The Future Speak Of A Bad Generation?

Don't like talkin' 'bout my generation,
It makes me ashamed to think of the bad,
We are the Devil's greatest creation,
We drive parents, teachers and the world mad!

There's some good 'bout my generation,
But now in time it is not very clear,
We shoot our neighbours while they're on their bikes,
Stab other people and bring about fear.

I want to be a good generation,
A small number of us already are,
With the right attitude and want of life,
We could change, we could go far!

Then people would speak in celebration,
When they're talkin' 'bout our generation!

Frances Bathurst (13)
Shaftesbury School & Sports College, Shaftesbury

What Is Life?

Do you ever think about how the world began?
What are we all about
And what's the aim of life?

Do you ever think about
Why the sky is blue?
Why do we have countries
And who are me and you?

Do you ever wonder what comes next in life?
Marriage, pleasure, what's our goal?
Before we part with breath.

Happy, sad what is death?
Why is it so scary?
Is Heaven heavenly?
Is Heaven hell?
What's life like above?

If Heaven is a party what's keeping them from dancing?
Is it seeing all of you cry over their dead body?
But when the crying and laughter stops what rolls through
                                                my mind is . . .

Do you ever wonder how the world began?

Josie Brownlee (11)
The Emmbrook School, Wokingham

When The World Ended . . .

Imagine a world without noise,
Not a bird singing . . .
Not a baby crying . . .
The silence was deafening,

Where once there was a proud city,
Now a dusty wilderness,
Crumbling buildings lay on the ground
Like a scene from a disaster movie.

Imagine a world without colour,
Barren and grey where flowers once grew,
The sky was a carpet of dust,
The sun was dead, there was eternal night.

Where once there was a flowing river,
Now a dried-up hole,
Dead fish scattered beneath the rubble
Only memories remained.

Imagine a forgotten world,
Where everything was dead,
Not a breath of wind in the air,
Hopelessness was all it had left.

The world's heart had stopped beating . . .

Alex Harvey (11)
The Emmbrook School, Wokingham

My Family

My family are amazing,
they mean the world to me,
each one of them is special just like royalty.

My mum is really pretty,
and quite funny too.
She is the best ever,
always there for you!

My dad is really funny,
and likes to make jokes.
He's a really special person,
and a super-cool 'bloke'!

My sister is like a best friend,
she's great fun to have around.
She's also quite pretty and clever,
not a better sister to be found.

Of course I have other family,
grandparents, aunts, uncles,
cousins as well,
all of them loving and kind,
they love me, I can tell.

My family are as precious as gold,
supportive in all that I do.
Their love surrounds me in a comforting hug,
I bet you wish you were loved this much too.

Danielle Murray (12)
The Emmbrook School, Wokingham

Badgers

We were a happy family,
Before they came.
They tore down our home,
They did.
They're bullies, they are,
Trying to tear down our home.

There was a crash and a rumble,
The children screamed.
Like mice we scurried,
Down the tunnel,
Through the darkness,
The time had come.

We almost lost Lucky,
We did,
He had only just learnt to walk,
But got him out,
Eventually,
But it took some heaving.

So now we're here,
In this revolting dump,
We do visit our old home,
We do,
But when we go there,
All there is, is hard black stuff,
And big monsters that go *brrrmmm!*

We were lucky to survive, we were,
But they're coming, nearer and nearer . . .

Hazel Gambles (11)
The Emmbrook School, Wokingham

The Rain!

The rain came pelting down on the windowpane,
I shouted . . . oh no, it's them again!
The monsters with the fingers as hard as steel,
Bang on the window,
In search of a meal!

Their cutlery ready for a crunch,
Their mouths ready for a munch.
Their plates the size of a dragon's lair,
Drifting leaves caught in their hair!

They stomped their feet,
And bashed their plates,
They all were bored of this tiresome wait.

They roamed around the garden bare,
I looked and saw nothing there.
I thought they'd gone for a minute or two,
Then I heard them bang and boom!

Suddenly,
The sky turned blue,
I stared outside and saw the dew,
No monsters there to devour me,
They'd moved on to find something else for tea!

Rachel Cox (11)
The Emmbrook School, Wokingham

The Extinction Of Animals

Animals living in forests are being killed by cutting machines,
Or murdering machines, as known to animals.
For animals their homes the trees,
Are exploding bombs,
And the animals are ants.

The humans are killing these poor, helpless animals.
They can't fight against this unstoppable power.
The forest of green is bulldozed red,
A sea of blood.

These innocent creatures are as helpless as babies.
The animals are like nails and the humans are like hammers,
Knocking them away.
The human race is a murderer.

If this continues,
All animals in forest habitats
Will become extinct.

Oliver Johnson (11)
The Emmbrook School, Wokingham

Changes

The tongues are sharp and the eyes are cold
The lips curl upwards, the brows will fold
The words fall out from a painted sneer
The creases form an unplanned leer
The girl, she crumples and hides her face
The bullies walk, they leave the place
She holds her hands up to rub her eyes
The black smears her knuckles and she cries
She scrambles up from her undignified fall
And clenches a fist, punches the wall
Head down, she walks, her hair a shield
From the outside world, she steps onto the field
She stops and stares and twirls her hair
She feels out of place, she doesn't belong there
Of all the names emo, goth, grebo and more
She does not care, but her heart is sore
But these things don't just happen, yes we all change
But it's people and incidents that cause the exchange
She's still the same girl but with black outlined lids
Which makes her one of those 'Emo kids'
No one can accept her, for they cannot see
Past the hair, the eyeliner, the jeans and the tee
Into her heart which beats just like theirs
And they cannot believe that she really cares
She doesn't smile every day, but it's really OK
Because when she smiles, it takes your breath away . . .
The eyes are creased, but they're sparkling
The lips curl upwards, smiling
The light on her face dances with life
And it is over, no more words, no more strife.

Laura Carter (13)
The Emmbrook School, Wokingham

Why On Earth!

Who are we?
What are we?
Why are we here?
We are like hopeless spies on a mission -
But what do we do?
Are we asking too many questions?
About the world we live in?
Should some secrets of this wonderful planet stay secrets?

Who's in charge of this vast kingdom?
Kings? Queens? Prime ministers? Presidents?
Who, we cry, who?
Who tells us all what to do to stop destroying the world?
No one. No one.

Global warming, we think we are safe from it
But it is a ferocious beast destroying the Earth slowly but brutally.
Ready to strike when we are most vulnerable.
But really we are the predators destroying habitats, melting ice,
Our car fumes seeping through the ozone layer,
Eating it away piece by piece.

Let's leave this poor world alone,
Be kind and gentle to it, don't ruin it or demolish it.
Carelessly in our day-to-day lives,
Let's help it and eventually it will help us too.

Megan Shillibier (11)
The Emmbrook School, Wokingham

The Lone Elephant

I am an orphan
My mother was killed
She was shot by a hunter
It was a worthless kill

I've sworn revenge
There is no forgiving
Forever the scar will burn
Never healing, never sealing

I will never forget him
The horrible man
He killed her for the tusks
I will hunt him like a lion

How long has it been
Without food or water?
Three weeks ago since the murder
I last ate three weeks ago

I cannot go on
In life much longer
I'm going to lay down here
And leave this horrible world.

Matthew Farndon (12)
The Emmbrook School, Wokingham

Beast Hunt

Smashing, bashing through the forest
Running for my life
Bullets coming this way, that way
It's raining death to me

Why, oh why do they want my fur?
Why does it have to be *me*?
Why, oh why isn't it someone else?
Why do I have to flee?

I had such a perfect life
No one ever stood up to me
If I wanted I took
That's the way it should be

But still I run and run and run
Never getting a rest
All my rights are gone
Trapped in a cage of injustice

And down I go, dead, gone, forgotten
Lost in all animal name
Man is meant to be smart yet
They cause so much destruction.

Harry Beasley (11)
The Emmbrook School, Wokingham

My Fantastic Family!

To have a family as special as mine,
You have to want a heart of gold.
To share your problems with everyone.

We giggle,
We cry,
We chat
Together.

My little sister can be annoying,
But really she means no harm.
She shares the world with everyone.

She fights,
She shares,
She plays
With us.

My mum is just like super mum,
She does everything we need.
She keeps everyone happy.

She cooks,
She cleans,
She washes
For us.

My dad works every single day,
He pays the bills we have to pay.
He is as funny as a clown.

He helps,
He treats,
He tickles
Us.

We do everything
Together!

Katherine Stubbs (11)
The Emmbrook School, Wokingham

The Sun Will Go Out

The sun's gonna go out,
It's got to some day,
It might be a million years away from now,
And I'll be long, long gone and forgotten,

But I've got a point,
One sharp point,
Sharper than a blade of a knife,
But I bet it will be long, long-gone and forgotten,

My knife is now like a shark's tooth,
So you wanna hear,
But my point is evil, my point is terrifying,
My point is evil, pure evil.

It is like an endless pit,
It is like Hallowe'en,
It is like a howling wolf,
But worse, much, much worse,

My point that will be forgotten,
Is *how will we get off the planet*?
Will some scientist save the world
Or will we perish?

Will we freeze?
Will we die with the sun?
What will we do?
I don't know, nobody does.

Anna Phillips (11)
The Emmbrook School, Wokingham

My Family

My family;
Well I guess they're OK
As I am with them
Every day

But trust me now
They're not that great
At times
Each one of them I will hate

I have one sister
Thank God that's all
For that girl drives me
Up the wall

There's Mum and Dad;
Well what 'bout them
I can't live with them;
Or without them!

But I mustn't moan,
Or even whine
Because basically
My life is fine

I've a house to live in;
Food to eat
Clothes to wear
And shoes on my feet

But without my family
I'd be alone
No one there
When I get home

That's why I love these guys you see
Because without them
It would be just
Me.

Jessica Phipps (11)
The Emmbrook School, Wokingham

My Best Friend Tris

I've known him all my life,
He's always there for me
When I'm feeling down,
He's my best friend.

His dog is as fast as light,
We play games with her,
We run away and she chases,
He's my best friend.

He's a demon in disguise,
He comes out
When people aren't around,
He's my best friend.

We go into town together,
Buy a lot of stuff
And travel home together,
He's my best friend.

He's two years older,
With eyes as blue as the sky,
I always am myself,
He's my best friend.

We go on shiny holidays,
He's also really funny,
I always see him,
He's my best friend.

He also has some chickens,
They cluck all the time,
They fly away if you scare them,
He's my best friend.

Elliott Jones (11)
The Emmbrook School, Wokingham

The Poor Boy

You are a cross
And I am a nought
Life's hard for me
And very short.

I live on the streets
All day and all night
I am usually nervous
And get into fights.

I get my food out of a bin
I don't want to steal
Because that is a sin
It's another tough day for me.

My parents left me a long time ago
My dad was poor
My mother was slow
They were the days they were in my life
. . . A long time ago.

I go to bed
Thinking of them
Under my smelly rag
Would they look over me
And see the life I have?

Nathan Onraet-Wells (13)
The Emmbrook School, Wokingham

Go Away

I wish they'd just go away,
Leave me for a precious day.
I want to run,
I want to hide,
I want to run away from my life.

They hunt me down,
Stalking me,
Just leave me alone,
Hear my plea.

I suffer in silence,
I'm so scared to tell.
It might turn to violence,
I'll hate that as well.

I wrote this yesterday,
But now it's all changed.
I told someone at school,
They're sorting it out,
I'm so happy I could dance and shout!

I don't want to run,
I don't want to hide,
This is the first day of the rest of my life!

Nadia Glover (12)
The Emmbrook School, Wokingham

My Family

There's my mum and my dad,
My sister too.
What they do for me.
We are one!

They see me safe along the way,
Happy as can be.
As loving as an angel.
We are one!

We're as happy as a winning team.
Funnier than a clown.
We all work together.
We are one!

We all help each other with
The cooking and the cleaning.
They are my best friends.
We are one!

They're the best thing in my life.
So special to me.
They're always there to help me.
We are one!

Ellie Horne (11)
The Emmbrook School, Wokingham

The Dead And Dying

Boom! As another bomb falls,
As fast as light.

All guns blazing,
As men fall like dominoes.

Children crying all around,
Mourning the dead.

Screams of agony echo
As death is welcomed.

The world turns as dark as night,
As smoke fills the air.

The stench of rotting carcass,
Float across no-man's-land.

Devastation stalks the streets,
Searching for its next victim.

The battle is over,
No one has won.

What a cruel place
This world has become.

Ben Brown (12)
The Emmbrook School, Wokingham

Black Roses

Red-hot tears brimming to the surface
Bubbling down like erupting lava
Looking out over a bleak grey landscape
Feeling hurt but distant like a single plane crossing the sky
The lonely feeling is suicidal
What is the point in living anymore?
Why not draw a knife, put an end to the pain?
She felt so weak
It was hard to breathe, why draw breath at all?
Confusion was spiralling down like fog
She was unsure where to turn
Every piercing look was a step back
A step down to unhappiness
She thought she was naive, innocent
If you dream hard it might come true
Imagination turned to reality
Deep inside she wanted to run
But knew it would bring no relief
Her smile was brief
She thought changing her style would change herself
But why dream? They will never become real
She was an emotional wreck of tears
Tears healed the pain, they splashed to the ground
Childhood ambitions destroyed
A normally happy disposition just a mask
You can't live two lives, you have to make a choice
Her life was slowly dissolving, it was out of control
She was living a life of lies
Every night she cried herself to sleep
The dreams yielded a little comfort in the dark hours of nothingness.

Becky Morrell (14)
The Emmbrook School, Wokingham

Dear Diary

Dear Diary,

Help me please.
You are the only one I can confide in.
A kind of only friend.

My friends just laugh it I tell them,
My enemies would laugh even more.
What if these things really happened?
I don't want to worry anymore.

What if something happens to my parents?
Then I'd be all alone.
What if they start abusing me?
Who could I tell?

I don't want to be bullied.
I don't want to be kidnapped.
I don't want my house on fire.
Won't these worries just let me be?

I'll call Childline.
No, it would be stupid to confide in strangers.
A teacher?
No, they're always too busy.
I know - my parents!
They're not strangers, they're never too busy, and they'd
                                        never laugh.

Yes, I'll tell my parents.
End of problems.

Becca Tizzard (11)
The Emmbrook School, Wokingham

Parkour Poem

As you stare down, to the concrete ground
A fall would make a deadly sound.
Getting ready to leap
Across the top of the street
You feel the thump of your own heartbeat

You practically fly
Over the sky,
Jumping from A to B
Balancing, swinging,
Vaulting and spinning
Then jumping from B to C

Cat-leaping
Pole-walking
Flick-flacking and more
Gaining a greater and greater score

As the day comes to an end
And you go round the last bend
Your legs begin to give way
So tired yet brave to escape from the grave
A hero was born today.

Mark Brown (13)
The Emmbrook School, Wokingham

Masked

At every flaw, a sudden jeer
Every shadow a lurking fear
Every hand that ever fell
A secret formed, they cannot tell
A masked face, a single tear.

Behind closed doors the string is pulled
She hangs the mask on the wall
Her smile was brief but fooled them all
The little girl with the mask.

Unspoken words she wished to say
Before the taunts were thrown one day
All the rain that ever fell
Couldn't drown her fears so well
Happiness lost its way.

Behind closed doors, sad looks she cast,
Gazing beyond the old, smeared glass
Awaiting the time the pain would pass
She still wears the mask on the wall.

Amy Allpress (14)
The Emmbrook School, Wokingham

Perfection

Great hair
Perfect face

You've gotta look great
Not just good, great
Kick-ass, the bomb
Trying to get to number one

Great top
Perfect watch

Check in the mirror
Blot your lips
Tightest belt
Shortest skirt

Great dress
Perfect earrings

Sheer tights
Designer shoes
Wobbling along
Mirror out again

Great shoes
Perfect scent

Let's face it
If you look like s**t
Who's gonna talk to you?
Not perfect, not popular.

Rachael Skinner (13)
The Emmbrook School, Wokingham

The Night You Went Out

That night you went out for tea,
You looked lovely and smelled like a rose,
The kids, tucked up safely in bed,
Or so you thought,

Won't be out for long,
You reassure yourself,
It's only across the street,
They'll be alright,
Or so you thought,

But while you're out,
Someone comes,
And breaks in,
Silently,
Swiftly,
Then they're gone,
Like a puff of smoke,

Then you return,
After a lovely meal,
To find them gone,
Your precious kids,
Gone,
Like little Maddie did,

You search everywhere,
Phone the police,
And question the confused neighbours,
But they're gone,
Just as you dreaded.

Ellie Phillips (11)
The Emmbrook School, Wokingham

Talkin' 'Bout My Generation

Acid rain,
Slowly,
Painfully,
Melts away the Earth.

Trees stripped bare,
By angry men,
Wanting space to build some houses,
All this just for money.

Earthquakes are destroying countries,
One by one,
All the land being destroyed,
Alongside all the people.

Hurricanes taking lives of the innocent,
Trees, people, animals,
Then we have to build it all over again,
Which usually involves creating pollution.

Take pollution for instance,
Someday it will get revenge,
On all of us who help melt away the glaciers,
It will also kill the innocent because of those guilty.

All of this is down to one person . . .

That person, is

You.

Casey Ward (11)
The Emmbrook School, Wokingham

Talking 'Bout My Generation

I'm afraid;
Afraid of terrorism,
Afraid of violence,
Afraid of drugs,
But what I'm most afraid of is my sister!
She's annoying,
She's bad,
She's like cold ice running up and down your back,
She's always there wherever you turn,
Her perfection is annoying,
Her life,
Her friends,
Her family,
She wants them all to be clones of herself,
I hate,
I hate,
My
Sister!

Katriona Gardner Whitney (11)
The Emmbrook School, Wokingham

Talkin' 'Bout My Generation

Just a normal day
Waking up to a splitting headache
The usual routine
Rolling up a piece of paper
Sorting out the white powder
Sniff . . .

Walking down the stairs in a dazed state
Opening the whisky bottle
But at the same time gazing at the unopened bills
A shiver going down your spine
As if a ghost had crept into the house.

Confused the emotional wreck puts on the ragged old clothes
They had worn for days on end
They squeeze their feet into shoes two sizes too small
Reaching for the front door they stumble over the mat
Covered in dust and dead insects.

No car to drive, they have to walk
The dreaded objects cover
What was once a good heart
With a black angry monster.

Liam Pietrasik (11)
The Emmbrook School, Wokingham

Maddie

Poor little Maddie been missing for months,
Her parents must miss her very much.
Kidnapped from the hotel bed,
Only at the age of 4, missing forever.

Is she dead, is she alive?
If she is she's got to survive?
In a dark, cold, grey world she cries . . .
Her tears cry tears and they do too.

Like an innocent prisoner in jail for no reason,
The poor, kidnapped, sleeping angel, missing forever.
Every child, every kid has nightmares of them being Maddie.
All that was left of the sleeping angel was a teddy missing its owner.

Pitter-patter go her tears on the stone floor she is kept on.
The place is a giant monster going to gobble her up,
Grey, cold, scary and confused,
All we want is her to be safe and back home.

Samantha Barnett (11)
The Emmbrook School, Wokingham

Bullied

Everybody's been there,
Been bullied, I mean.
You'd just be standing there, not doing anything and then you'd
hear them calling.

I mean, I don't mind the names,
However rude they may be.
Well, OK, I'm lying,
I hate them all the same.
I ignore them as I walk past
And keep my head held high . . .
. . . But after, when I stop and think
I *always* want to cry,
It makes you think you're being singled out,
I mean what did you do to them?
It's not like you've offended them,
It's just the way you look and dress.
I guess that's it, really,
You feel like you've been hit,
Every time they do it,
It eats away at you and then you find,
That you just want to disappear.
I swear this world is going wrong.
No, no, I'm being serious,
Because when you stop and think about it,
This world is all the same.
It's not based on your intelligence,
Or your personality,
It's just the way you look and dress
And that's what is so sad,
I guess the world just wasn't built,
For a person just like me.

Stephanie Jacqueline Kent (12)
The Emmbrook School, Wokingham

London Bombings

I was at school when I heard this dreadful news
About terrorists bombing London
I'm thinking how dreadful for people on the trains

It makes me feel sick thinking about the bombs dropping from the sky
Boom, boom, boom
And the sirens around London

People screaming, people crying
Loads of people hurt
I just think to myself, *why?*

No one could get anywhere
All roads closed
It was a long day

People ended up with no arms
No legs, no feet and even paralysed
I'm sorry for the families
Who experienced the
London bombings.

Mitchell Webb (11)
The Emmbrook School, Wokingham

Friends

Funny as monkeys,
Playing all the time,
Running wildly round the park like dogs off their leashes,
Flying swiftly like birds into the tops of the trees,
Chasing each other like a non-stop Ferris wheel.

Saving the world again and again,
Destroying all evil,
Wiping out the enemy,
Leaving the opposition far behind,
So we can cheer in victory.

Having massive parties with all your mates,
Getting new toys and games,
Imagining crazy stories and tales,
That scare the daylights out of you,
And we all like having fun.

Aaron Scicluna (12)
The Emmbrook School, Wokingham

My Family . . .

My family; we are so strange,
First of all there's my sister - she's sort of cool,
But we all need to change.

Also there are the brothers,
They could be better - they could be worse,
Pay me please, I am in a curse.

My mum, my dad, they're not that bad,
They buy me clothes,
I also have some socks for my toes.

When we are all together we make *sooo* much noise,
Especially those ridiculous boys,
We may be big, we may be small,
But we are all for one and one for all.

Sarah Colbourn (11)
The Emmbrook School, Wokingham

Talkin' 'Bout My Generation

In Iraq trouble is brewing,
Troops are leaving; they are told that the work is done.
If the work is done,
Why is Iraq in every newspaper and splashed across page to page
in magazines.

We've sent out the RAF,
The Royal Navy,
And the army; but we still can't hold the insurgents back.

Is there a problem with our army?
Is there a foil in our plan?
Is it time for the troops to come home
Or do we need to help Iraq more?

Was it a good idea to invade in 2003
Or should we have stayed out of their business?
Some say yes, some no . . .
The right decision no one will know.

Josh Pymble (11)
The Emmbrook School, Wokingham

Talkin' 'Bout My Generation

It was doomsday 9/11.
Every hard-working person went to work that day.
Most of them lost their lives.
For a reason that is stupid.
Why?
People screaming, shouting, calling for help.
But only the people near the bottom floor survived.
They jumped out of the windows,
So that they didn't suffer.
Then . . .
It fell, all was silent.
The shouts and screams.
People who had lost loved ones.
Why?

Maximillion Crowhurst (12)
The Emmbrook School, Wokingham

Bullying - Haikus

Where is teacher now?
I need someone to see this,
As punches rain down.

They think I am fine
But I'm not, it hurts me so
As punches rain down

Should I tell someone?
They say, 'I shouldn't or else'
As punches rain down

I did not give them
The money as they'd asked me
More punches rain down

Help me teacher please
They hurt me every day now
And punches rain down

So now it has stopped
They sent them away from here
No punches rain down.

Will Shillibier (13)
The Emmbrook School, Wokingham

Terrorism

If only terrorists would go away,
Then everyone could go out and play,
Maybe even for only a day,
'Cause we're the ones who always pay

They make people die in flight,
So no one can have a good night,
We could be playing with a kite,
While someone else will have to fight

But even when they're caught,
I knew they would surrender or so I thought,
And then they'd come back with new force,
But if they did so would we of course

They will never stop,
And they will continue to chop,
Until we surrender or kill them all,
They will always make our buildings fall.

Tom Peterson (11)
The Emmbrook School, Wokingham

Cruelty To Animals

What is that? Is that a cat,
Sitting on the mat?
But look at it; it's cold and wet,
It looks like it should see a vet.
And look, it's got no collar on,
It looks like it's been thrust upon,
A cold, dark, dirty street.
That cat was treated badly,
And now I must say sadly,
That it may not see the light,
After tomorrow night.
As it will not live long,
That's why cruelty's wrong.
To take a poor cat's life
And make it die in sorrow,
Knowing it may not see tomorrow.

Natasha Keane (13)
The Emmbrook School, Wokingham

Birthday

B ursting with excitement
I t's nearly time
R eady for my party
T oday gonna
H ave lots of fun
D anni and
A nnita are here
Y ay, it's my
S pecial day.

Bronwyn Annetts (12)
The Grange School, Christchurch

Being Young Means

Being young means
Being in love
Having lots of girlfriends
Kissing in the dark

Being young means
Going to school
But to me it is such a fool
School is such a bore

Being young means
Getting a job and learning to drive
Going to school unless I skive
Trying to act well.

Jack Frampton (11)
The Grange School, Christchurch

Dancing

D o a dance
A ny dance
N ot a tango
C an't do a waltz with extra spins
I like to join in
N ine to ten kicks
G reat dance.

Kiera Barton (11)
The Grange School, Christchurch

Death - Haiku

Dragon breathing death
over every town it sees
nothing is alive.

James Baron (11)
The Grange School, Christchurch

Being Young Means

Having fun with your mates
Being young means
Getting bullied
Being young means
Going to new places and doing new things
Being young means
Having new friends and pets
Being young means
Playfighting with your mates
Being young means
Having to look after your little sis
Being young means
Being sick on a Saturday
Being young means
Being dissed by your sis
Being young means
Watching scary movies with your mates
Being young means
Going to school!
Being young means *not getting your own way!*

Jade Rowing (11)
The Grange School, Christchurch

Shimmering Snowflakes

Shimmering snowflakes glitter in the sky
Pitter-patter on the window
Glistening in the light
Dancing on the ground.

Children in the street playing in the snow
Running around, all around
Pitter-patter, pitter-patter
How long will it last?

Annie Malla (11)
The Grange School, Christchurch

When I Grow Up

When I grow up
I think I'll be
a swimmer
in the ice-cold sea

I could be an author
or an astronaut too
I might be an actress
and be on Dr Who

I might own a chip shop
and serve them fried
I'll be a scout
and then a guide

I'll be a train driver
on the Underground
I'll be a rock star
with lots of sound

For the more a girl lives
the more a girl learns
I bet I'll be most of these
by taking turns.

Katie Sida (11)
The Grange School, Christchurch

Football

F rank Lampard crosses
O ver to
O sman who
T oe punts it over the
B ar
A ll of the team
L augh and shout
L oser.

Peter Wedge (12)
The Grange School, Christchurch

Being Young Means . . .

Being young means you don't have to go to work
and you don't get wrinkly,

Being young means getting lots of homework
that's OK but not the best,

Being young means having a best friend
and an enemy,

Being young means big school
where there are lots of bullies,

Being young means having fun,
going shopping with mates,

Being young means you wish to be an adult
but you're still young,

Being young means you can let your mind
go off in its own little world,

Being young means you get help
from the teachers with your work.

I love being young!

Alice Burton (11)
The Grange School, Christchurch

Being Young Means

Being young means we have sleepovers with all the girls,
Midnight feasts and watching scary films,
We talk about boys and shopping.

Being young means being in love and having girly talks,
We love to have chocolate,
And we love to talk about sleepovers.

Being young means going to school,
Which ain't cool,
And being such a fool.

Chelsea Heanes (12)
The Grange School, Christchurch

Being Young Means

Having to go to school, getting lots of homework,
Getting lots of DTs
And getting bullied.

Not being wrinkly,
That's very good,
Then you don't have to wash in-between the wrinkles.

Being young means playing games all through the day,
Going on the computer all night,
Going to bed late
And getting lots of toys.

Rhys Daniels (11)
The Grange School, Christchurch

School

Gran wakes me at the crack of dawn
A day of boring school is about to begin
My uniform is uncomfortable and annoying to put on
I hate all of my lessons except for my early gym session

I beg the teacher to let me free
And I am able to get out of my DT
Hurrying home to change into my own clothes
Meeting my friends in our little spot.

Callum Gooch (11)
The Grange School, Christchurch

Being Young Means

Being young means going out every night
getting bumps and bruises
and always up for a fight.

Being young means playing video games all night
winning all the time
and always up for a fight.

Being young means going to school every day
coming home at night
and always up for a fight.

Being young means having homework every night
And always up for a fright.

Jordan Perry (11)
The Grange School, Christchurch

Being Young Means . . .

Waking up early, eating my breakfast,
cleaning my teeth, going to school,
not being allowed to drive,
having detentions,
hanging around with my friends,
I get toys.
Being young is pretty cool!

Zac Tilsed (11)
The Grange School, Christchurch

In The Water - Haiku

Looking at water,
my reflection scares me as
it's what I've become.

Eden Warne (12)
The Grange School, Christchurch

Pressure

My mum is ill
I'm under pressure
My dad is hurt
I'm under pressure
My sister's too young to take care of
I'm under pressure
My brother's either at work or college
I'm under pressure.

Stacey Murphy (12)
The Grange School, Christchurch

Funderworld

We had a great time,
not causing any crime,
the sun was shining,
I thought to bring,
my lucky thing,
but in the end I had my friend
who is always there,
never gave me a silly glare.

Lauren Hood (12)
The Grange School, Christchurch

Graffiti

G reat effects
R espective colours
A dditional black and
F rightening yellow running
F ast as we can
I can still see the colours
T urning around
I am so amazed.

Levi Ridealgh (11)
The Grange School, Christchurch

I Thank You

If I talked to you
Would you answer back
Or would you just
Sink silently into the black?

If I could look at you
What would you say?
I would listen faithfully
While your worries melt away.

If I could hold your hand
Would you pull away?
I'm sorry if I hurt you
Let me make it all OK.

If I ever said anything
To wound your soul
I know your feelings have been broken
As time took its toll.

If I could just sit down
And write a love song
I'd write it for the person
Who made me sing for so long.

I know it's not that easy
To just pick up the pieces
Cos all I left behind me
Was destruction and diseases.

I guess that we weren't perfect
Darling, you and me,
But I just want to thank you
For making me a thousand times what I used to be!

Amy Stenner (12)
The Ladies' College, St Peter Port

Refugee Boy

I feel so vulnerable and alone,
So out of place with no home,
I'm just a poor refugee boy.

It makes me ever so sad,
When I think of my lost dad,
I'm just a poor refugee boy.

My mother is long dead,
From a bullet to her head,
I'm just a poor refugee boy.

The soldiers destroyed all our land,
And from the town we were banned,
I'm just a poor refugee boy.

Gunshots fired loudly in the air,
People killing without a care,
I'm just a poor refugee boy.

The war is out of control like a raging fire,
This isn't the life that I desire,
I'm just a poor refugee boy.

A man comes over a blue helmet upon his head,
A helping hand and a smile he will spread,
I'm just a poor refugee boy.

His kind words take away my despair,
At last I have found someone who really does care,
I'm not just a poor refugee boy.

Eden Staples (12)
The Ladies' College, St Peter Port

The Last Person On Earth

Being the last person on Earth is hard,
No one is there to send you a birthday card.

The Earth has been destroyed,
Only you have survived.

The golden leaves dropping from the sky,
As you walk across the autumn air and sigh.

Unaccompanied in the end of this world,
Everything silent, only your footsteps could be heard.

The trees waving their branches like arms,
Little flowers glowing like little charms.

Giving you some hope to live
And some hope to survive.

Crunch, crunch the leaves go,
As each of the leaves are touched by your tender toes.

Suddenly you let out a yelp,
Because your foot has been jammed in a trap and you
need some help.

Your foot has been bleeding with rushing blood,
Flowing out rapidly just like a flood.

Suddenly everything goes blurred before your eyes,
And in your vision the floating feelings rise . . .

Sunaina Reddy (12)
The Ladies' College, St Peter Port

When I Grow Up!

When I grow up I'll be the boss
Make people do everything for me
I will, but hopefully people won't hate me
So no, I won't be that

When I grow up I'll be a pilot
Do the loop-the-loop and flip upside down
But hopefully we won't crash, then they might not like me
So no, I won't be that

When I grow up I'll own a shop
Sell sweets and pie only
But then the parents might get mad
Shut me down
So no, I won't be that

When I grow up I'll . . .
Do whatever I want
I won't let people boss me around
Yes, I will be that.

Erin Renouf (12)
The Ladies' College, St Peter Port

My World

If I could create the world
I would have gingerbread houses.
Sugar-coated trousers
Purple liquorice grass
Chocolate-coated sea bass
Marshmallowy trees
But I would not recommend . . .
Sweet and sour peas.

Sophie Morellec (12)
The Ladies' College, St Peter Port

Perfection

Am I too big, am I too tall?
Going out, being out, wear my best
Am I bigger than the rest?

Am I too skinny, am I too small?
Going out, being out, don't breathe
1, 2, 3, 4, heave and breathe

Am I too brown, am I too pale?
Going out, being out, try to do my best
The fake tan is my quest

What am I like in this top?
What am I like in this skirt?
What am I like in this outfit?

What will my friends think?
What will everyone else think?
Will they all hate me?

Hang on, my friends are my friends
And who cares what everyone else thinks
Nobody's perfect

So wear what you want to wear
Be who you want to be
'Cause perfection has never and never
                                    Will
                                       Exist.

Laura Stoddart (12)
The Ladies' College, St Peter Port

In The Cold Crisp Snow Of Lapland

Outside, the cold crisp wind
Crackled the leaves from the trees
And the rabbits hopped through
Cold winter's night snow.

The whipping winds of St Nicholas' night
Pounded the roofs, then silence
There was soot on the floor and ripped wrapping paper
Outside a purple coat and sleigh.

St Nicholas slumped in a pile on his sleigh
The presents were out and ready
But he was still stuck in the snow
With many miles to go.

St Nicholas found himself in
The snow of Lapland, where else?
And set up camp with cute dancing elves
With hooked noses and stripy clothes.

He settled down, made Lapland his home
With a new name of Santa Claus
And thanks to Coca-Cola,
New dress sense of red and white.

Ellie Taylor (12)
The Ladies' College, St Peter Port

Differences

I lie alone, divorced from the world.
They lock me away to hide me.
I am too different, too unique.
They say my imprisonment isn't for long, but it is forever.
Apart, away, unwanted, unloved.

No one will talk to me, so I sit alone.
There is no point to my existence, they say.
They leave me, drowning in blood and tears.
I'd change if I could, but I can't.
I feel nothing, I am nothing.
Despised, different, neglected, unloved.

This feeling will ruin me.
My senses have died completely now.
The blackness is rushing up to me.
Is this death taking mercy on my scarred soul
Or is that too much to hope for?
Shunned, invisible, discarded, unloved.

I feel as though I'm free now, no boundaries surround me.
The darkness has come and gone as I prayed.
Now, I can see that there is nothing to fear.
Death comes to all and I have been taken.
I feel happy for the first time, happy!
Reborn, roaming free, thankful and truly alive.

Elizabeth Reynolds (12)
The Ladies' College, St Peter Port

The African Child

Every day when we wake up
A poor African child is suffering.

Every day when we eat our breakfast
A poor African child is starving.

Every day when we travel to school
A poor African child is working.

Every day when we are working at school
A poor African child is education-less.

Every day when we are eating our lunch
A poor African child is looking after their younger siblings.

Every day when we are doing PE
A poor African child is crying in pain.

Every day when we are having fun with our friends
A poor African child is homeless.

Every day when we are doing maths
A poor African child is being a slave.

Every day when we are going home
A poor African child is dying from AIDs.

Every day when we are sleeping
A poor African child is being helped.

Laura Oxburgh (12)
The Ladies' College, St Peter Port

Tony Blair

I stand here now
Alone
In the corridor of power.
Everyone waiting outside
Cameras flash, journalists shout.
This is my exit and I look back at my entrance.
Did I do enough?
Could I have done more?

In 1997, that spring when all were joyous and our new world
was Camelot.
I had won their confidence and promises of education,
Less crime, stop poverty and stop the bad things.
It was a fragile start and soon the money flowed and everyone
was happy.

Then a cloud - a shuddering stop that shook the country
And the world, the death of a princess.
I called her the people's princess.
And with Europe we tried to have the same money - the Euro,
but Gordon knew better and stopped me.

Then, the worlds changed, September 11th 2001 New York,
Death from the skies, my heart sank, it grieved me.

The Americans were angry, as angry as a lion with a thorn in his paw.
I prayed and God said, 'We must fight against the terror and the fear.'
The people looked up to me!

Bush and I linked arms and sent the army.
We knew that Saddam had nuclear bombs, or did we?

Now, 5 years later, it looks like a mess in Iraq and people have said
That I must go.
Was it all my fault?
Was I the Americans' puppet?

They are asking me to solve the problem in Lebanon now.
Can I? Will they trust me?
I don't know - but my heart is strong.

So now I take my last steps out of the door of 10 Downing Street.
A new world for me today.
Will I be remembered just for Iraq or for the good I tried to do?

Sometimes trying to do your best is like making a sandcastle
When the tide is washing in.

So, bring on the tide today, tomorrow, whenever. I will keep
Building castles.

Izzie Sheil (12)
The Ladies' College, St Peter Port

The Words That Haunt

The words that haunt,
Are they real?
Do they bring out the dramatic scenes?
Do they lie or tell the truth?
You cannot be sure as darkness grows near,

You think of these words,
Does it mean death is near?
They wander round your head,
Haunting you in every space,
Does it mean life is at its end?

Can you be sure it is not just a trick,
Lowering you in,
So there is no way out?
You cannot climb back out,
Because darkness has just began.

There is only one way to bring light again,
That is to have faith in the role you play.

Samantha Carter (12)
The Ladies' College, St Peter Port

Our World

Have you ever wondered what
the world would be like without life?
there'd be no terror, stress or strife.

The world would be empty
with nothing to grow.
Was it like that at the beginning?
We'll never know!

The world would be silent,
nothing could be heard,
no laughter, no shouts,
not even a word.

The world would be colourless,
no rainbows there,
the great artist of the sky,
would be in despair.

The world would be horrid,
so barren and bare,
God would look on the world and say,
'Who wants to live there?'

Louise Vivian (12)
The Ladies' College, St Peter Port

Who Am I?

Who am I?
Am I the leaves on the tree?
Am I the clouds in the sky?
Am I the fish in the sea?
Am I the moisture in the air?
Am I the stars in the darkness?
Am I the water when it rains?
I am impossible to explain
I'm not small but tall
I'm a bit of it all!

Natalie Hadley (12)
The Ladies' College, St Peter Port

Questions For Life From A Child

Is life to question
Or is it there to live?
Were wars supposed to happen
Or was it someone's arrogance?
Was the Titanic supposed to sink
Or was it an accident?
Do people always wonder like me
Or is it me asking questions?
I know a lot of things, but not nearly enough.

Is the world going to melt
And is doom on the horizon?
Do aliens really exist
Or is it just the scientist bluffing?
Am I asking too many questions
Or is it my imagination?
We all work for money and for life,
So can we work together and do what is right?

Abigail Corbet (12)
The Ladies' College, St Peter Port

Being Homeless

I wake up, I'm starving to death,
I wake up, I'm getting stared at,
I wake up, I am freezing,
I wake up, I'm getting sworn at,
I wake up, I've been given a coat,
I wake up, on a hard bench,
I wake up, it's been raining,
I wake up, I'm being killed,
I wake up, I'm looked down on,
I wake up, I've nowhere to go,
I wake up, I'm getting thinner,
I wake up, I long to be loved.

Rebekah Fant (12)
The Ladies' College, St Peter Port

What Would The World Be Like If . . . ?

What would the world be like
If wars kept on?
What would the world be like
If love was gone?
What would the world be like
If people didn't care?
What would the world be like
If no one was there?

The world would be horrid
If these were true
The world would be horrid
So what should I do?

The world would be better
If we didn't fight
The world would be better
If we used our might
The world would be better
If wars stopped
The world would be better
If poverty was chopped

The world would be lovely
If I made these true
The world would be lovely
If you helped me too.

Nicky Bourne (12)
The Ladies' College, St Peter Port

Open Your Eyes

Open your eyes
To cries of the children
Starved of salvation
Tears fall from the sky

Open your eyes
To the fall of a soldier
Struck out in battle
Love pours from the soul

Open your eyes
To the shouting and screaming
Running with terror
Fear eats them away

Look at our world
So ruined, so rough
The people are fighting
To make them seem tough

But it's wrong
This isn't what God made us for
The suffering, the hatred
The blood and the gore

Just open your eyes
Dig into your heart
Pull up the courage
And we'll make a new start.

Flinty Bane (12)
The Ladies' College, St Peter Port

The Young Black Stallion

(This is a story of a young and loved stallion)

The girl walked up to me and touched my face
She looked into my eyes. 'I'll call you Grace.'
Then she got in my field and said to me,
'You're the most beautiful stallion I ever did see!'
She stroked my long black body and smiled,
'Why are you so perfect and yet so wild?'
She climbed on the fence, I started to pace.
'I'm going to tame you Amazing Grace!'
I had no clue what she was doing, I was getting very scared.

My eyes were glowing with fear.
'Come here stallion, here!'
She beckoned me to the fence and I gradually got closer.
'Come on boy, just a little bit more . . .'
I had to trust her, she was so gentle,
But I didn't know what I had in store . . .

I lined my body up against the fence,
She gave me a pat and I relaxed.
She climbed upon my back and held on to my mane.
What was she doing? I started going insane!
She nudged me with her feet, 'Whoa boy, steady!'
She sat firm, tight and upright on my back, calmly patting me.
Letting me know I was safe, I calmed.
She got a Polo out of her pocket and handed it to me gently.
I sniffed then ate it very delightfully.
By now we had a very strong bone,
We rode round my field and I drank by the pond.

It soon got dark and she had to go home,
'I'll come back soon Grace, I promise!'
She left and I didn't see her for two years, I had lost all hope . . .
I saw a face in the distance, it was her again!
I neighed with excitement; she got on my back,
'I promised,' she said.
With a good Polo and a pat on my neck we galloped off,
How I loved my life!
This girl I knew, she was gentle, kind, amazing . . .
Mine!

Emma Baxendale (12)
The Ladies' College, St Peter Port

All Alone Through A Horse's Eyes!

In my field I eat and eat as if I'm starved,
That's all in my field, all alone,
No friend or family,
Only the dead grass and me.

Every day they bring me into my dirty stable,
Where I stand and stand.

Then a saddle is thrown on my back,
And a bit, harsh in my mouth,
Someone leaps on my back,
Tugs at my mouth,
Kicks my stomach
And makes me gallop and gallop away.

Across the hard fields,
Over prickly hedges like a field of brambles,
Twigs brushing my skin like daggers,
The pain, the misery.

They think I enjoy it,
No horse could enjoy that torture,
But I have to gallop on and on,
Till my feet are dead and the moon has shone.

They take me to what they think is home,
I stand in my dark, damp stable,
With no food, and only dirty water,
Why don't they just leave me alone?
In a wonderful land of my own,

They put me out in my same old field,
I eat again and again till my mouth is sore,
I'm free like a bird but so alone,
I carry on eating through the dark night,
Waiting for the next lonely day to come along!

Freddie Best (12)
The Ladies' College, St Peter Port

It's Not Always Easy, Being A Dog

'Rufus! Rufus!' I hear my mum cry,
So I decide I had better half-open one eye.
There, in front of me, she stands,
My beautiful mum, with a bone in her hand!

Excited as I could possibly be,
I go over to her and she hands it to me.
Then, out into the garden I trek,
Carrying a bone this big is giving me a sore neck!

Just as I start to chew my delicious bone,
Horror strikes - my dad is home.
Yelping with fear, I look around, where should I hide?
Under the trampoline is where I decide.

But it's no use, he's running towards me so fast,
Oh how I wish he would forget the past.
He's got a shoe, oh no, please God, no,
As he comes closer my fear starts to show.

Usually I would run away at this stage,
But today I am frozen with fear and rage.
He hits me with the shoe, ten times, very slow,
He is shouting whilst going from blow to blow.

Finally, Mum calls him indoors,
As he goes, I fall to the floor.
Just wishing he would never do it again,
Although wishing doesn't work, it's worth a try now and then.

So I hope this will make you feel for dogs like me,
And remember being a dog is not always easy!

Amber Buckingham (12)
The Ladies' College, St Peter Port

The Stallion

I was caught from the wild when I was two years old,
I miss those happy days of freedom.
I am black with big green sparkling eyes.

My owner is horrible, he whips me into doing things,
it doesn't work though.
I only listen to the stable boy Tom.

He rides me every day except for Sundays when he goes to church.

When he rides me, it's like nothing else in the world,
we gallop for miles upon end with the wind lashing in our faces
and ducking under the branches which seem as if they are trying
to knock Tom off.

My favourite part of the gallop is when we get to fairy stream,
Tom squeezes me and I leap as high as I can over the stream,
clearing it by a mile.

When I am ridden Tom whispers words of encouragement
into my ear,
They are always kind words, never spiteful.

Our gallop ends when we near the green lane,
he walks me so I can catch my breath.
'There's a good lad' is one of his favourite expressions.
I love to hear these words, but I never do from my owner,
he's a hard man . . . I hope he never sells me.
I mean nothing to him but everything to Tom.

Charlotte Brooksbank (12)
The Ladies' College, St Peter Port

My World

If I was born just before God the world wouldn't be the same.
Sweets and clothes and the Earth would have a different name.
Pink land, sweet land or maybe smile land, happy sort of things.
There would be diamonds and lipstick and piggies with wings!
We wouldn't travel in polluting old cars, bubbles instead.
We would float round and never go to bed.
There would be school but no papers and pens.
We'd use computers and emails we'd send!
No veggies, no fruit, enough of that.
No wasps, no bees and definitely no rats.
No school books, magazines are much better.
We'd be so caught up in emails, no time for letters.
It would be perfect, no wars, no stress
I couldn't wish for anything less.
Oh wait, what is this, a list of complaints?
My bubble just popped, I'm blinded by bright paint!
The pink is too much, I'm getting too fat
My pony just died, I miss my old rat.
The clothes just don't fit, they all hiss!
I'm getting too tired, I've had enough of this!

Helen Monachan (12)
The Ladies' College, St Peter Port

A Blind Man's Tale

Darkness, never-ending,
Blinding, like a cloud of smoke,
Columns of darkness, clouding all view,
Visions gone, only pitch-black ahead.

But you know, know people are there,
Hear them, smell them, feel their presence,
They laugh, you can hear them,
Knowing that they are laughing at you.

Old and crippled you stand at the roadside,
Not knowing which way to go,
You stumble and fall, but no one cares,
No time for the old blind man.

No one to love you, no one to care,
Alone in the world ahead,
You cry and you shout and you scream to the world,
No time for you, they couldn't care less.

But then someone speaks, kind words they say,
Take you by the hand
And warmth and care and comfort you find,
Love for the old blind man.

Sian Brodrick (13)
The Ladies' College, St Peter Port

Life

Life is a journey to the end,
Out to reach your destiny,
Every step you take,
Every corner you turn,
Makes another page,
In your story of life.

Life is a jigsaw puzzle,
Waiting to be put together,
At first it is confusing,
But then it's worked out,
And every piece fits perfectly.

Life is like a tree,
At first it needs lots of care,
But as it grows,
It can look after itself,
And every leaf is like a memory.

Life is like a box of chocolates,
You never know what you're going to get,
So many choices,
So many options,
It will work out in the end, you'll see.

Life is a roller coaster,
Swooping up and down,
Some scary parts,
Some fun parts,
But it reaches the end too fast.

Dannie Jones (12)
The Ladies' College, St Peter Port

The Way You Move

I see you walking down the street
wearing those new high heels.
Going to work in the café
serving all those delicious meals.
You're the one I dream of
you're the one I will choose
because the thing I love about you
is the way you move.

I go sit down in the café
wanting you to serve me.
I order fish and chips
with a nice cup of tea.
You're the one I always stare at
you're the one I will choose
because the thing I love about you
is the way you move.

My meal is now over
I'm ready to pay the bill.
You're standing there with another man
kissing behind the till.
You were the one I once loved
you're the only one I would choose
but the moral of the story is
I loved the way you moved.

Kirsty Bynam (12)
The Ladies' College, St Peter Port

A Tiger's Life

My
First
Sight of the world,
Green grass,
Animals charging about,
And the soft orange and blackness of my striped fur.

I get up on my weak legs and take my
First
Steps.
After a while I run about,
Play with my brothers,
We growl and we shout.

The day starts to end,
I look up to the sky to see my
First
Star surrounded by a black blanket.
I close my eyes,
And fall asleep dreaming about my next day.

As dawn breaks I start to wake up,
I hear a gunshot,
Turn to see what it is,
I see my mother,
Being carried by an ugly creature,
And she's on a sharp hook.

I run and I run as scared as can be,
For hours maybe days,
Then I reach my destiny.
Loads of other tigers,
My brothers and my friends,
I decide to stay with them until the end.

Evie Domaille (12)
The Ladies' College, St Peter Port

A World For My Children

A world for my children,
Is that too much to ask?
A world with no war, no hatred
Can't we all get along for a while?

A world for my children,
Is that too much to ask?
A world with no bombings, no terrorists,
Alas.

A world for my children,
Is that too much to ask?
A world with no cruelty, no tears,
A bit of love and respect is what they need.

A world for my children,
Is that too much to ask?
A world with no cruelty, no tears,
A bit of love and respect is what they need.

A world for my children,
Is that too much to ask?
A world with no loss, no thieving,
But for one to give and another to receive.

A world for my children,
Is that too much to ask?
A world with no murder, no rape,
Nothing to make anyone sad.

A world for my children
Is that too much to ask?
A word with no deforestation and no animal slaughter,
A world where we are all one.

A world for my children,
Is that too much to ask?
No, not now we know . . .
. . . The dangers of life!

Laura Corbet (13)
The Ladies' College, St Peter Port

Wrong Place, Wrong Time

I saw the look in his eyes,
He was going to kill.
I felt something inside me,
But I didn't know what it was.

When people are about to die,
They say they see their whole life,
Pass through their mind and relive it,
But it really wasn't like that.

I was frozen to the spot,
Knew I should move, but couldn't.
I saw him tighten his grip,
On the gun pressed against me.

I thought of my family,
But knew my time was up.
I looked up at him, in the eye,
And whispered, 'Do it quickly.'

I waited for what felt like hours,
Breathing the last of my air,
Thinking each breath was my last,
The final beat of my heart.

What had I done to deserve this?
Really, I was innocent.
Just in the wrong place, wrong time.
I didn't even know this man.

Just twenty years of age I was,
Hard-working but up for a laugh,
Hadn't had my fair share of life,
Seriously, this wasn't fair.

I glanced down, the gun was still there,
Pressed tightly to my thumping heart.
Then slowly he squeezed the trigger
And *bang* my life was over.

Lydia Collas (12)
The Ladies' College, St Peter Port

Homage To Hiroshima

As I fly, I remember
The way my ancestors flew,
High above the valleys,
Singing their song to the world.

As I fly, I remember
The way the landscape once was,
Rolling hills, trickling streams, blossoming cherry trees,
A land at one with nature.

As I fly, I remember,
The way the city was filled with life,
Daily hustle and bustle,
Countless radiant faces.

As I fly, I remember,
The planes flying, high above the city,
The noise of their endless whirring motors,
The end of an era.

As I fly, I remember,
The blinding light, the blast.
I remember a shockwave,
Rippling through the land.

As I fly, I remember,
The way the city died,
In one moment, taking with it
Countless radiant faces.

As I fly, I remember,
The way my ancestors flew,
High above the valleys,
Singing their song to the world.

Rhiannon Carys Jones (12)
The Ladies' College, St Peter Port

My Barbie World

So here I am in the cupboard,
I last saw daylight five years ago,
There is dust all over me
And mould is starting to show.

The kids sit on their laptops now,
Chatting on msn all day,
I really wonder why they keep me,
They might as well just throw me away.

I much preferred when the children played with me,
Rather than leaving me here all alone,
I preferred it when they were carrying me around,
But they replaced me with a mobile phone.

I wonder what the world's turning into,
With all the terror and the bullies and the fear,
I am still sat here in the cupboard,
The children are so far yet so near.

Lauren Buckingham (12)
The Ladies' College, St Peter Port

The Beach

Beautiful sunsets in the water,
That look exactly like my daughter.
The calm gentle waves remind me of
Her tears that dripped onto my shoulder.

The sand reminds me of her soft hands,
That used to stroke her dog called Dan.
Each brown pebble in the sand,
Reminds me of her chocolate brown eyes.

And every time I come to this beach,
I remember my daughter
Looking into my eyes and saying,
'I love you Daddy and I love this beach'.

Jessica Fiore (12)
The Ladies' College, St Peter Port

The Fear Of The Knife

We live in a world full of strife
Living in the moment with the fear of the knife
Parents young, old and wise who live with the grief
From their children who have died.

We should be able to believe
Those children will be safe tonight
With the people they love alright.

That promise can't be made
But parents and people sit and pray
Sometimes this turns into dismay.

We beg you to think today
About the parents that live this way
We come together to display
The way we feel about that day.

Elinor Freestone (12)
The Ladies' College, St Peter Port

Gorilla

I am hunted
I am killed
I have no home
No one knows how many we've lost
No one knows how we feel
No one knows the loss we've grieved
Everyone knows that we are related
But the hunting goes on.

Emily Martel-Dunn (12)
The Ladies' College, St Peter Port

If I Were Prime Minister

If I were Prime Minister,
I would change the world,
In as many different ways as possible,
For the good of all mankind.

Global warming,
Gun crime,
Endangered wildlife,
And energy-saving projects,
Would all be on my agenda.

I would aim to end poverty,
In all developing countries,
Giving everyone food and clean water,
Every day of the year.

Global warming,
Gun crime,
Endangered wildlife,
And energy-saving projects,
Would all be on my agenda.

I would try and stop wars starting,
So everyone could have a peaceful life
And feel safe in their home country,
That is their human right!

Global warming,
Gun crime,
Endangered animals,
And energy-saving projects,
Would all be on my agenda,
Because I want to make a difference.

Rosie Davis (13)
The Ladies' College, St Peter Port

Generations To Come

The sky is pink
It makes you think
Houses are green,
And things are clean.

People are nice,
No melting ice,
The gulf stream is still there,
It took lots of wear.

The Earth did not warm,
The Devil was not born,
People all recycle,
And everyone has a bicycle.

But now the time has come,
My job has been done,
The Earth will be great fun,
For generations to come.

Abi Howard (12)
The Ladies' College, St Peter Port

Waiting

Sitting on the dry, soft, yellow sand,
Thinking that one day I'll be home,
Waiting for someone, just waiting.

Watching the ocean glisten in the sunlight,
Letting the breeze blow my hair side to side,
Waiting for someone, just waiting.

My body roasting in the bright sun,
My throat dying of thirst.
Waiting for someone, just waiting.

One day I hope with all my heart I'll be home,
Free from this hot, deserted island,
Waiting for someone, just waiting.

Francesca Bachelet (12)
The Ladies' College, St Peter Port

Through The Eyes Of A Blind Man

I am blind

A ngry sometimes
M issing my old life

B right sunshine
L ush green grass
I nk on paper
N ight skies have
D isappeared forever

N ow my hands are my eyes
O pening the world to me
T ouching life

H elpless I am not
E very day is easier
L ove surrounds me
P eople who care
L etting me live
E njoying my company
S eeing past my blindness
S eeing the real me.

Alice Davis (13)
The Ladies' College, St Peter Port

The Case Of The World

The world is filled with people,
Of many kinds of race.
We need to keep together,
To discover our case.

But still there is hatred,
Violence and war.
We think we are right,
But just break the law.

Our hearts of stone are solid,
We need to share the love.
Make peace with one another,
The symbol, a dove.

Break our stony hearts,
No more hatred by race.
To be with each other,
So we can discover our case,

Of life.

Lisa Marquand (12)
The Ladies' College, St Peter Port

A Girl

A girl who is frightened,
Do you know her name?
A girl who is beautiful,
Seems to always take the blame,
But happiness comes and goes,
But still we have sorrows.

A girl from a land of fairies,
Does she even exist?
A girl full of tears,
With scars on her wrist.
These things that I say,
Are they true?

Or

A girl who is frightened,
Do you know she exists?
A girl who is beautiful,
With scars on her wrists,
But happiness comes and goes,
We still have more sorrows.

A girl from a land of fairies
Seems to always take the blame,
A girl full of tears,
Do you even know her name?

Kate Friedlaender (12)
The Ladies' College, St Peter Port

Abandoned

Left in the streets to shiver and cry,
Not knowing if I'll die.
Kicked out of my house for no apparent reason.
What's going to happen?
Will I ever be found?
The sun goes in and the moon comes out,
My tummy growls and my ears go down,
I'm just a little dog with nowhere to go.
What will I do?
Where will I go?
What's going to happen?
I'm cold, I'm hungry,
I've nowhere to go.
It's raining, it's pouring,
It's dark and it's cold.

I'm abandoned.

Emily Maindonald (12)
The Ladies' College, St Peter Port

Pressure

Today, I was alive
Come a normal day
Yesterday was the same
Though tomorrow was different

It all changed so quickly
More trust, then sense
Friends should be true
But Devil in disguises

Two-faced ways between them
Plotting, for what it takes
Clever and sneaky underneath
Smiles and lies on the skin

Sinister but persuasive
Effective but pure cruelty.

Ollie Shrimpton (16)
Uplands School, Poole

Talkin' 'Bout My Generation

My generation has to go to school.
I hate homework and always do it at the last minute.
I meet up with my friends
And that's school for me.

My generation is funny about food.
Vegetables and fruit are disgusting.
I eat pizza, chips, ketchup etc . . .
Fast food is the best.

My generation likes to spend its free time in front of TVs,
PlayStations and computer games cannot be beaten.
But too much time spent always leads
To arguments with Mum and Dad.

My generation loves to play sport,
Getting muddy is what I do
When playing football and rugby.

My generation is the best
Because it's when you get mobile phones
And when you get to meet up with your friends
After school.

Aston McCarthy (12)
Uplands School, Poole

My Poem About My Generation

Life, rhythm, soul, music
It affects gangs, people, who we hang out with
And it lets you express who you are
And what you like.
It shows emotion, you can cry, love, dance, sing along.
The list is endless,
Everything is connected to it.
What clothes you wear, what make-up you wear.
Even who your friends are.
It plays a massive part in our generation.

Aimée Guichard (13)
Uplands School, Poole

Talkin' 'Bout My Generation

Shopping one would love to do,
Special occasions so much fun,
Dressing up in your greatest attire,
Having your nails and hair done.
Maybe a game of whichever sort,
Being a board game or the best PlayStation.
Your mobile phone you can't live without,
The computer - not even to be discussed!
Some of us sporty,
Tennis or netball.
The boys ridiculously into their football.
A trip to the cinema to see the latest film,
Gathering of friends, popcorn and all!
Your friends seem the most important in your life,
Spending all your time with your one and only best.
Told off by your parents,
It doesn't seem that big a deal.
But then you realise you should listen to their advice!

Lillie Cohen (14)
Uplands School, Poole

My Generation Of Drugs

In my generation I daily see teenagers taking drugs.
But are drugs good or bad?
The start of it could depend on the situation.
It may seem cool but it won't in the end.
Do not get tempted if you want to live,
Temptation could be deadly.
Using drugs to rest for a while could end up being an eternal rest.
It's hard to stop once you start.
So stay strong, not physically but mentally.

Otis Ooi (14)
Uplands School, Poole

Talkin' 'Bout My Generation

Whether it's a Saturday in town
Or a day at the beach,
No matter what, your friends are always in the picture.
When the bell rings on the last day before summer
Everybody goes crazy!
Endless days at the beach or shopping on a Saturday.
No more school for the whole summer.
No one our age could live without their phones or the Internet.
Lazy mornings tucked in bed,
Music is a must
And shopping is the best.
Going for a stroll with friends
Or spending all evening on MSN.
My generation always has fun.
Your mum constantly nagging you
To tidy your room,
And not doing any homework.
Going back at the end of summer,
Everyone missed their friends.
Running up and hugging them.
'It's been too long,' people say to each other.
Sitting through boring lessons,
Giggling to one another!
Yes, it's the weekend, at the end of the day on Friday.
Seeing friends, shopping or cinema, or beach or sports.
No matter what our generation will have fun!

Bianca Arden (14)
Uplands School, Poole

My Generation

My generation seems to have everything!
iPods and PSPs.
We communicate electronically.
Mobile phones and MSN
Bebo and E-mail.
New styles of speech and new styles of text.
It's Gr8 2 b kl!
Teenagers still love their music.
Hip hop, rock and metal!
Watch their favourite bands on MTV.
At school not much has changed,
We wear uniforms, eat school dinners.
Too many tests and exams.
SATs and league tables.
Some things are worse.
More bullying, more drugs.
More assaults on kids.
Not much freedom for teenagers.
Parents worry too much.
'Don't talk to strangers!'
'Mind the road!'
'Don't walk home alone!'
Teenagers spend a lot of time alone in their bedrooms.
Maybe my generation doesn't have everything.

Jack Fuller (14)
Uplands School, Poole

My Generation

My generation is technology,
My generation is about learning new things,
My generation is about media.

There is sports, maths and English,
French, Spanish and art,
But these we learn at school.

Bad things like war,
Terrorism and yobs,
But in the end we are just humans.

You can ask the question
Why?
But it doesn't have many reasonable answers.
It's just our generation.

Jack Webster (14)
Uplands School, Poole

The Day I Was Chaved

Life is light whilst death is dark
Life and death are one alike
A teenage life

As a knife pierced into my flesh I felt lonesomeness
As the dark blood skipped from me I felt emptiness
As the sharpened fan sliced me I felt frostiness
As I was falling to darkness I felt breathless
As I was failing to exist I felt uselessness
As my life attacked me I felt shameless
Now I was gone I felt shadowless

As I looked up I saw the one who had taken me.

Anoush Fard (15)
Uplands School, Poole

My Generation

My generation, cocooned in violence and hatred,
Its lack of respect for authority, adults
Or, for that matter, anything living or dead.

My generation, infamous for its insensitivity
To buildings, chairs or anything that remains
Stationary or intact.

My generation, a gun in a pocket and
A knife at hand,
Rampaging beneath the glare of flickering street lamps.

My generation, peering out of the haze
Of smoke and hallucination
A raging fire inside their minds.

My generation, full of it,
Stuffed to the brim,
Hairs and hands glistening
With oil from their polystyrene meals.

My generation, a facade to reality and humanity
With no depth, no character, no feeling.

Shadman Chowdhury (15)
Uplands School, Poole

Generation . . . Why?

G angs, a new problem, guns that exploded in '07
E minem, our modern-day poet, when he's gone just carry on . . .
N o more film, memory cards now 100s on a card
E ducate yourself . . . Teachers not required!
R educe your carbon footprint in your hybrid car
A mazon.com, books still rule
T errorists, Bin Laden, *tht evl bgger!*
I nstant messaging, WUBU2 TLK L8R M8 . . . BiBi!
O nline shopping delivered to your door.
N uclear testing, Iran don't go there.

Your problem . . . and mine!

William Smith (15)
Uplands School, Poole

Talkin' 'Bout My Generation

We want Xbox 360, PS3 and Wii!
Fast games
Not the slow black and white films.

We want sports cars, motorbikes, quad bikes!
Fast wheels
Not old cranky Rovers.

We want hard rock and pop!
Fast music
Not boring classical.

We want freedom!
Fast life
Not rules and homework.

We want pizza, chips and Coke!
Fast food
Not broccoli and Brussels sprouts.

We want South Park!
Fast TV
Not Coronation Street.

We want respect!
Not old fogies glaring at us
Telling us what to do.

We want to be heard!
To have a voice!
And to be listened to
Not to be looked down upon.

We want
Fast!
Freedom!
Fairness!

We wanna have fun!

Frank Morley (11)
Uplands School, Poole

Talkin' 'Bout My Generation

Bang, bang, bang!
Mum wakes me up,
Sister's on the computer,
Mum going on about her generation,
'We never had computers in our day!'
Get with the 21st century Mum.

Walking to town,
iPod turned up,
Mobile phone rings,
Get a text from Dad
Not very good at it though,
Worthless attempts at shorthand,
Bless him.

In town with my mates,
Mum gave me a tenner,
'Don't use it all at once,' she said.
But I spend it on lunch and sweets all day.

Back at home
Mum's doing the dinner.
'How was it in town?' she says.
'Not bad!'
'What did you spend your money on?'
'Sweets and food!'

Kids these days . . .

James Stone (15)
Uplands School, Poole

Girls

The love I have for girls is of high value,
It's the only reason why my heart is beating.

Girls send me into such bliss,
Their hair radiant like the warming sun,
Their eyes more beautiful than the stars in the sky.

Their lips more - more loving than roses
Their hips so well shaped, like a juicy tropical fruit.

The love that they give to me,
Makes me feel like I am floating above the clouds.
It makes the butterflies in my stomach
Want to burst out in happiness.

Now that I am in love,
The trees smile at me,
The waves that crash on the coast have a better rhythm.

I cannot control my emotions,
They are too overwhelmed by love.

I know not of what my future with love is,
But I do know that,
Girls are like my light switch,
They turn me on.

Byron Russell (15)
Uplands School, Poole

Speechless

So many things you think you'll never do,
Saying to yourself, 'They won't make me do that,'
But you and I both know;
One day you will do whatever it takes to fit in,
To be like the people you see on TV.

> You want to make yourself
> Noticed and heard
> But when it comes to it
> You're just left speechless

Sitting at home watching the news,
Thinking, *not all teenagers act like them,*
But you know some of your friends do,
You don't want to be another stereotype.

> You want them to know
> You don't think it's cool,
> But when it comes to it
> You're just left speechless.

We're put into categories because of our age
Or the way we look,
But one day people will realise
That's not what matters.
What matters is who we are within.

Hollye McKenzie (15)
Uplands School, Poole

The Notion Of Eternal Motion

We wonder not about the clouds who are the prisoners of the sky
We gaze not at the ripples that are bound to the water
We care not about the leaves who are the inmates of the trees
For we are captives of the screen in front of us
Not at leisure with the beauty that surrounds us
We look only forwards and not behind
Learning only multiplication and division
Not the meaning, consequence or sacrifice
Though what is youth but motion?
And motion comes with the danger of chance
Like a train on the rails that others before us have laid
It is easy to derail and fall
But to be raised back on it takes grit and determination
Not least by those who choose to carry you
We care for everyone except for others
And not even for ourselves in times of temptation
As we live only for the moment.
However we do not realise that other's moments will arrive
And they may be more fruitful for our actions
But the notion of Utopia is simply not human
As all this like the clouds . . . the leaves . . . and the ripples
Will never change.

Ben Rogers (15)
Uplands School, Poole

Mind The Gap

I keep an eye on the gap;
As your ambivalent journey continues.
It's a long, long way from Brighton to Brixton
'Cowboys and Indians' to cold-blooded murder.

Carriage 1; small boys in the park
Jumpers for goalposts.
Carriage 2; small boys in the park
Smaller boys for targets.

You can lay a track to redemption, nevertheless
You are laying the track closer,
And closer to the end of the Earth.
You lay the track
And
You ride it out

I've lain mine
But still.
I keep an eye on the gap;
As your ambivalent journey continues
And my unfaltering journey comes to an end.

Robert Kerr (15)
Uplands School, Poole

Emotional

My room normally darkened at midday,
Thoughts of misery and death creep in,
My generation is full of hate and anger,
And black make-up and fringes.
I weep with tears of desperation,
Cos my father is missing at sea,
For how I dream the war will soon die,
Unlike Father.

But a shining light through my curtain has entered,
My cuts are healing and now I see
How I can better myself.
I rang up Matt to meet at the local park,
We smoked ciggies and raged on about our fringes.
Both of us are getting a new haircut.
We threw away our make-up and emo CDs, and cast them asunder,
Tears of desperation are no more,
For I have seen the light.

Daniel Giles (15)
Uplands School, Poole

My Generation

In my generation
There are jets soaring around in the sky.
In my generation
Global warming is dangerously close to destroying the polar ice caps.
In my generation
There are terrorists destroying London.
In my generation
There's England beating everyone in the Rugby World Cup.
In my generation
There are loads of animals becoming extinct.

Piers Anderson (12)
Uplands School, Poole

My Generation

Over all these million years everything has changed
New technology has been made such as
Computers, televisions and mobile phones.

My generation has mobile phones so that we can
Contact other people to have a conversation.
We also have computers so that they can help our work
Whenever we have troubles with something.
Finally we have television so that we can enjoy
Watching programmes and news.

We have computers, televisions and mobile phones which is good
But having all this stuff doesn't always make our life fun.
I must care more about my education and
I must not always rely on my computer
I must do sport as well so that I will be healthy and
                                        have more stamina.

Max Ooi (12)
Uplands School, Poole

School

School.
The word sends a shiver down my spine.
The word means hard work and foul dinners.
It means manic teachers, horrid exam papers
And evil headmistresses.
But sometimes, there is a light at the end of the tunnel,
For at school we have the best thing imaginable -
These people help us when we are in need of assistance,
Or let us copy work when we are stuck.
They are friends.
So maybe I can struggle through the work and torture at school
If I have friends there to help.

Oliver Jagger (11)
Uplands School, Poole

My Generation

Standing in the playground,
Chatting with my friends,
Laughing out loudly,
The fun never seems to stop.

Listening to music,
Phone in my pocket,
Chatting on the computer,
We always seem to be together.

Money, money, money,
That's all people want
But give me friends any day
The talking never ends.

Friends, talking and technology
Now that's my generation.

Rebecca Baxendale (12)
Uplands School, Poole

My Generation

My generation,
Filled with games,
Mobile phones,
PlayStations,
PSPs,
DSs
And other electrical devices.
My generation,
Filled with ice cream,
Chocolate, dark and white,
Sweets that make your teeth rot,
Coke that fizzes you up
And coffee that is disgusting!

Sam Harbord (12)
Uplands School, Poole

My Generation

My generation, my generation,
People think wrongly of me,
My generation, my generation,
They say I am bad.

My generation, my generation,
I am a defenceless child,
My generation, my generation,
I still go to school.

My generation, my generation,
Though sometimes I may not do well,
My generation, my generation,
I will get it in the end.

My generation,
My generation,
My generation,
People look down on me.

Pavlos North (12)
Uplands School, Poole

Talkin' 'Bout My Generation

A tsunami of technology
Sweeps us into this age of instant communication.
A deluge of e-mails clogs up our computers
Drains away our energy.
As polar ice caps melt, we switch on our phones
And text and play games.
Our land floods,
We watch DVDs, TVs, Nintendo, Wiis.
We switch off.

Daniel Sharland (12)
Uplands School, Poole

My Generation

It's up to us to keep our planet together
Let *my* children see the polar bears and penguins
Let them see them for real
Not in a book or a TV channel.
Cut greenhouse gases
Walk to school, turn off lights, recycle.
Let our carbon footprint be small.
We need to care for our environment now
. . . before it's too late.

Techno-logy
Techno-land
iPod, i-computer, i-phone . . . I wonder?
What new skills we've had to learn.

What about bagatelle, marbles, knuckles and jacks?
What about climbing trees, making camps and just mucking about?

Never mind, I'm too busy styling my quiff and perfecting my image.
But hey that's my generation!
G-g-g-g-eneration.

Chris Brewer (12)
Uplands School, Poole

Homeless

Homelessness is in my generation,
It is upsetting and hard work.
You see it everywhere, it's almost like you never don't.
We look down at them and feel disgusted
But how would we like to sit in the cold
With no TV, MP3, iPod or anything.

We are lucky that we get presents
Homeless people try to keep alive and warm
Whereas we can't even think about being cold.
So next time you see someone homeless
Think how lucky you are
And then you'll know your parents do it for you.

Katie Pearce (12)
Uplands School, Poole

My Generation

In my generation the technology is phenomenal,
In my generation the food is incredible,
In my generation there is global warming,
People are rich and poor in my generation,
People are fit and healthy in my generation,
Children *are* seen and also heard in my generation,
Taxes are quite high in this generation,
People are kind in this generation,
People are also evil in the 21st century generation,
In the 21st century generation holidays are booked
                              and go ahead as planned,
In the 21st century generation, people are greedy,
This generation is about power and politics,
This generation has different sorts,
Generations are changing in good ways and bad ways
And I hope this one changes in a good way.

Lucy Carter (11)
Uplands School, Poole

OAPs Takin' Over My Generation

Oldies think they're better,
They think we're total trouble.
Oldies would do better sitting knitting knickers,
They're always tired and grumpy.
Oldies think they're better, something's got to be done.

Oldies look down their nose at us,
They make us look 'up' at them.

They shout at us if we yawn!
They fume at us if we slouch
And how many times have you heard the line
'Children should be seen and not heard!
Shh! Quiet! Sit still! Don't scratch! Eat with your mouth shut!
Sneeze in a hankie! Don't look at me like that Madam!
Don't Breathe!'

Emily Condie (11)
Uplands School, Poole

Doormat

Why do they think it's okay to stand on me?
Maybe I forgive too easily or just try to see the good in people.

Why do they think it's okay to stand on me?
Maybe I should create a wall around me, to keep everything away,
What right do they have to push me about?

Why do they think it's okay to stand on me?
Do they not think I have feelings?
They stomp around not realising the damage.

Why do they think it's okay to stand on me?
What goes around comes around
Because this doormat has found its feet and learned to stand
And will be walked on no longer.

Bethany Williams (15)
Uplands School, Poole

My Generation

Grannies always thinking we're hooligans
Telling us to get off the pavement
But my generation is not like that
It's about having fun.

Old peeps think I'm wasting my time
On videos and computer games
Well they're wrong, it's great fun
It helps hand-eye co-ordination.

My generation is the future of the world
Older people disagree
The future depends on us.

Andrew Power (12)
Uplands School, Poole

My Generation

In my generation fat people rule the streets
In my generation everyone has mobiles
In my generation you can't turn around without seeing a chav
In my generation kids spend hours in front of the television
In my generation school is a chore
In my generation food isn't a problem
In my generation most people have electricity
In my generation you send emails not letters
In my generation the Internet is a part of everyday life
In my generation you are always being watched
In my generation no one uses CDs anymore
In my generation you always have light over you
In my generation fast food is more popular than proper food
In my generation we are starting to worry about global warming
In my generation we are running low on fossil fuels
In my opinion my generation is still the best!

Wesley Glover (14)
Uplands School, Poole

My Generation

My generation has hamburgers and junk food and takeaways,
So we can eat all day long.
My generation does hip-hop dancing and loves it.
We have jet-skis to ride the waves
And laser lights to light up the sky.
We have computers which we call PCs.
We have mobile phones to contact our friends day or night.
My generation has skateboards so that we can roll our way to school.
We don't ever get bored because we have video games and
                                                    fight imaginary monsters.
Wouldn't you like to belong to my generation?

Cassidy Ooi (12)
Uplands School, Poole

Talkin' 'Bout My Generation

Technology is my time,
My age,
My place.

Mobile phones are smaller,
Way smaller than bricks.
iPods are modern
Replacing cassettes.

Technology is my time,
My age,
My place.

Harry Potter was published
Took over the world
Have you seen yourself on YouTube
Or Googled the Earth.

Technology is my time,
My age,
My place.

Come live with me in my time
And be a tourist in space.

Beth Dooley (11)
Uplands School, Poole

Bullying

Bullying is mean
Bullying is wrong
Bullying hurts people's feelings
Bullying is calling people names
Bullying is making fun of other people
Bullying is looking down on someone
Bullying is making people feel afraid of you
Bullying is making people small inside
Bullying makes people not want to tell the teacher
Bullying is wrong.

Emma Smith (12)
Uplands School, Poole

My Generation

Cool hairdos,
Cool clothes,
Smart thinking
Is my talent.

A glass of champagne,
Or down to the pub,
I don't care which,
But I'd rather have the better one.

Fast cars,
Hot wheels,
Speeding round the park.

Laptops, computers,
Gamestations, iPods,
And mobile phones.
All part of my generation.

Alasdair Burn (12)
Uplands School, Poole

My Generation

Things have changed over the years,
Including people's lives.
When TV came out they thought it was good.
Now parents think it's bad.
So much technology has come out,
Now it's brainwashing us all.
Long sea trips have turned into flights,
Swords have turned into guns
And we can travel to the moon.
What next? Living on Mars
Or a tree that speaks for itself?

Matt Holland (12)
Uplands School, Poole

Defeat Is Not An Option

Like all fourteen-year-old schoolboys of my generation
I love the challenge and the test, the chance to prove,
To see if I am the best and can win against the odds
Gamers will unite tonight, to play and fight electronically
Our modern world uses the magic box – the Xbox 360!

All hobbies need to change and grow with the times
A while ago skateboards were our passion, the ultimate
                                              sporting fashion
Now we are soft and like our thrills and spills on the screen
The range of games to play is vast and full of innovations
Whether it is sport or battles we love to beat our mates.

This age has created the 'geek' and 'computer nerd'
The 21st century has reached out across the globe
Through the ether you can challenge and communicate
                                              across the world
Bikes and sports are still the bread and butter of our lives
But, our age has a lot more to offer – good or bad, you decide!

Jeremy Bond (14)
Uplands School, Poole

A Life Of Crime

Everywhere I look I see a life of crime,
If it isn't on the news it's in front of me,
Life is one great crime that we all live each day,
We can't go through our lives without seeing a crime,
As we look at our world we realise that we are ruining our lives,
Our generation is looking full of surprises,
New angles on life are opened and closed,
We look at our lives and think of what it could have been,
A life we hope to live is just around the corner,
Every chance for our generation to escape life's crime is closer
                                              than it seems.

George Fullerton (15)
Uplands School, Poole

Talking About My Generation

Adults rushing across the street
Because they are late for work.

Teenagers skulking around street corners,
Smoking and eating chips.

Children going mad for the latest computer game
Shouting at their parents.

Toddlers running in the park with kids they've just met,
Acting like they have been best friends for a lifetime.

And babies coming outside with their mothers
Seeing things they have never seen before.

That is my generation.

Jaina Vithana (11)
Uplands School, Poole

Chavs

People wonder why I hate them
Maybe it's the fact that they can't wear hats
Or even the fact they tuck their trackies into their socks.

Could it even be they think they are seven feet tall
Or maybe they think they are the hardest thing ever
Next it could be they wear big fat rings from Argos.

It could even be because they have to destroy everything
Maybe they get girls pregnant when they are thirteen
Or they drink beer for breakfast.

Finally they think they are cool because of the happy slap
Or maybe they have to steal stuff for drugs.
Maybe it is because they think they are God's gifts to women.

Dan Pritchard (15)
Uplands School, Poole

Generation Deceased

Thinking about times,
Times change and become different,
Times are ghastly or excellent,
Times are filled with complexity.

Opportunities pass for happiness,
Happiness from wooden toys,
Happiness from books,
Happiness from television and gaming.

Happiness or sadness,
Sadness from disease,
Sadness from slavery,
Sadness from wars far away.

Hard times become easy,
Easy for us to have recreation time,
Easy for us to have luxury food,
Easy for us to survive.

What is making this how it is?
How is it possible that not all are equal?
Why do things change for better or worse?
Is this even reality?

There is something,
Something which can assist us,
Something which can hinder us,
Something which has the power for transformation,
The transformation of the generation.

Toby Adams (14)
Uplands School, Poole

Talkin' 'Bout My Generation

Pressure to pass
Pressure to succeed
Pressure to be cool and hip
Pressure to fit in
Pressure to belong
Pressure to love
Pressure, pressure, pressure

What if I don't pass?
What if I fail?
What if I'm not cool and hip?
What if I don't fit in?
What if I lose everything?
Where do I belong?

What if, what if, what if . . .?

This is my generation.

Tom Evans (14)
Uplands School, Poole

My Generation

My generation
Is cool and fun.
It's all about PS2s and playing footie.
My generation is about jumpin' around
And watching TV.
My generation is all to do with
Riding bikes and playing sports.
My generation is about having friends
And being friendly.
As I get older I will do different things
But always be in a generation.

Liam Meakin (12)
Uplands School, Poole

Talkin' 'Bout My Generation

Going to the skate park
Listening to my iPod while I'm walkin' around the town
Talkin' to my mates about the latest football scores.

Searching through Bebo to see who I can find
Any hot girls on line?
Playing on my Wii and my PS3.

Talking to my mates on MSN
Should be doing homework but I'm sending emails instead
Getting really late, I must go to bed.

Too much homework, too many tests
I could do without the stress
I'd rather be watching South Park.

That's what I like to do!

Alex Wyer (11)
Uplands School, Poole

Truth

When the day is over
And you look back on what you have done,
Can you honestly say you are pleased,
Satisfied with the day just gone?
Do you feel you have won the battle
Or long ago lost the fight,
To fulfil your dreams, your ambitions,
To make something of your life?
Or are you like the rest, all around
With your feet stuck firmly on the ground?

Jonathan Summerell (14)
Uplands School, Poole

Exciting Generations

Lots of people come and go,
Leaving nothing behind,
Generations come and go,
But they leave commodities behind.

Generations convey different products,
Like the mobile phone,
Some previous generations
Brought along TV.

In my generation
Many objects have been invented
Like the Nintendo,
And the PS3.

I love my generation,
The whole caboodle, more than I could possibly dream of.
This poem should be passed down
Generation to generation.

Lauren Talbot (12)
Uplands School, Poole

My Generation

Bullying is in my generation,
It happens a lot,
It happens all the time,
Especially when you're my age.
It happens everywhere, in every country and town,
It will never stop,
But something is being done
That is what I know of.

Bullying is a way to threaten and frighten others,
And a way to abuse and hurt people's feelings
It can also make the person feel hurt and very upset.
That is what is happening in my generation.

Roseanna Au (12)
Uplands School, Poole

Gadgets

Nowadays there is hi-tech this,
Hi-tech that.
Lots of things are now
Electronic or computerised,
And lots of people want everything up to date.

Some things are portable,
Some things are small,
Some things are big, and
Some things are medium-sized.

New things are coming out all of the time,
As soon as you get one gadget
Another one comes out.

They are just like cars,
Different ones are coming out all of the time.

They are always being improved
And being made better.

Lots of things in the world,
Are trying to be made better.
And some people are trying
To make the world better as well.

Megan Hallowes (12)
Uplands School, Poole

My Generation

My generation is full of super new things,
From new machines to hip hop music.

There are tons of sports like football and rugby,
Swimming and long jumping.

But the best thing of all
Has to be man's best friend, TV!

Oliver Gristwood (12)
Uplands School, Poole

My Pictures

Pictures on the wall, the first one I see.
It is in different colours, shapes and sizes.
It looks like a colourful sky set by the sea
With a villa just by the water.

Pictures on the wall, the next one I see.
It looks like a paintbrush scattered across the paper.
I thought it looked like fireworks on the beach
Going up into the sky.

Pictures on the wall, the last one I see.
It stares into a daydream.
It scared me once, I thought *it's got to be Hallowe'en*.
I looked up again, I was so right.

That was the end of pictures
I never saw them again.

Lauren Bungay (12)
Uplands School, Poole

My Generation

My generation is full of technology
and worries about the next trend.
My generation is helpful
it helps people in wars.
My generation has lots of fast food
but it doesn't feed the homeless.
My generation is full of fun things
but does not care for the environment.
My generation spends billions every year
and everybody has the latest games.
My generation spends all day in the car
and it drives me crazy.

James Heslington (11)
Uplands School, Poole

Talking About My Generation

The brain of the TV lies in the remote,
Too many channels to see at once,
From reality to shopping,
From sport to cookery,
I prefer watching 'The Simpsons'.

Ebay is the world's largest shop,
Millions of things to buy and sell,
From pencils to cars,
From holidays to gigs,
I like looking for games!

Mobiles are wireless communicators,
Texting, calling, radio and music,
From Samsung to Blackberry,
From Bluetooth to infrared,
I have a Sony Ericsson.

Facebook is a new cyber website,
Too many people on it to count,
From sharing pictures to chat,
From nudging to poking,
I prefer Myspace.

Nintendo Wii is a new games console,
It is movement controlled,
From graphics to gameplay,
From sport to shooting,
I like playing tennis and golf.

Jake Redrupp (12)
Uplands School, Poole

My Generation

My mum always says,
'You kids get so much more these days.
It's not like it was in my day.
From PlayStation to Bebo,
Mobile phones to Sky Plus,
iPods to Limewire.
You kids don't know
How lucky you are.'

So I asked about her generation,
She said, 'Vinyls, Pacman and Duran Duran.'
I looked blankly at her,
She put me in her arms and squeezed me.
'OK Mum, don't go overboard.'

My generation is super fast,
Always a new PSP game for sale
Or a new website to browse.
Did you update your profile on Bebo
Or download Ne-Yo's latest song?
I've got to have the latest baseball boots
Oh, and the new Now CD.

Are we a generation that is ever happy,
Or a generation that always wants more?
I say, in any generation
It's family and friends that count
And at least in my generation
You can keep in contact with friends
And family . . . instantly
No matter what part of the world they live in
So . . . I like being in my generation!

Ariana Woolrych (12)
Uplands School, Poole

My Generation

Is my generation really that different?

Yes, we can communicate without wires,
entertain ourselves with video games,
shop on the Internet,
and send a text on a mobile phone.

Yet, we still enjoy the simple things in life:

Eating good food,
being with our family,
listening to music
and having some quality time with our friends.

But, we still have the same problems:

Dying from diseases,
quarrelling with our friends,
and fighting pointless wars.

Robert Bell (12)
Uplands School, Poole

Evolution Through Time

Slings and swords a millennia ago,
Goliath fell, as gladiators rose,
Rexs and fish the size of the moon,
Until she ventured and wiped them to doom!

'Time is the best medicine,' my mother once said.
'Patience is a virtue,' my father once said.
I say we ponder until our turn comes,
My father went and then my mum,
A disco, a ball, at the prom?
Sprawled opened, perhaps the heavens?
This is my generation 2K7.

Anthony Skilton (16)
Uplands School, Poole

No Milk And Cookies

The games we once played
. . . seem so long ago now.
Our dusty shoes and forbidden secrets
. . . which never lasted.
I wince back on the toke of my cigarette
placed delicately between my first two fingers;
The signature sign.
Do not judge me passer-by,
do not stare speechless at reality -
Fool.
I will roll up my skirt and sip on your booze,
this is what you asked for.
I try to gain the last bit of youth,
tapping my heels together
. . . just like Dorothy.
You took away our milk and cookies,
we cannot play anymore.

Eileen Stone (15)
Uplands School, Poole

My Nana's Childhood

Going to my nana's makes me think
of what it must have been like when she was my age.
No iPods or mobiles,
no computers or TVs.
Only board games and sketch books to play with.
They didn't have as many cars and different ways of transport
as we have now.
She couldn't talk to friends on the phone or MSN either,
but Nana says she didn't mind not having all the technology when she
was young.
She still had a great childhood
and thinks kids nowadays get too much.

Savannah Townsend (13)
Uplands School, Poole

The Growing Problem

Heat temperatures rise and ice caps melt,
Water rises and disasters strike.

It is a growing problem.
It is causing icebergs to shrink,
We watch as polar bears tire and die,
We read about penguins choking on oil that they have swallowed
Due to oil ships crashing into underwater icebergs.

We aren't able to reverse the process,
But we can slow the process down to save our children's
And grandchildren's lives.
All it takes is for the world to work together.

In our generation we are all in peril,
If nothing is done, then humanity will have no choice
But to wait until our weather change condemns belief.

Global warming is the growing problem of today.

Casey Fullerton (12)
Uplands School, Poole

Communication Madness

My generation live with their mobile,
My generation love their mobile,
My generation would die without a mobile,
My generation would be nowhere without their mobiles.

Our parents' generation lived without mobiles,
Our parents' generation wrote their messages not texted,
Our parents' generation would die without a pen,
Our parents' generation would queue outside payphones.

The future generation will have brain implants,
The future generation will be telepathic,
The future generation will have no mobiles or pens,
The future generation will never *stop,*
Madness lasts *forever!*

Liam Mather (14)
Uplands School, Poole

My Generation

Gaming is great,
Gaming is fun,
Gaming can be an illness,
For adults and for kids,
Games are just fine,
For fun and with mates,
So watch what you play,
And you'll be OK.

Alcohol and drugs,
The sickness of the Earth,
People are suffering,
For food and for water,
Which we all take for granted,
The world can be an unfair place,
And that is my view on what the world has become.

William Evans (13)
Uplands School, Poole

Selfish Generation

My selfish generation, and how we don't appreciate,
What comes easily in life?
Food, water . . . and television
People one hundred years ago
Had to strive for these things,
Televisions were only for the ultra-rich
But now to us selfish things
It comes easy!

Oliver Williams (15)
Uplands School, Poole

When You Were Young

How can so much change in so little time?
When yesterday it was building dens among fallen trees,
out in the open, with fields and fresh air.
It was only forty years ago when you were running free up and down
your street,
Hair running wild, skirt muddy and not a single threat.
When not long ago you were playing elastic gymnastic in
back gardens,
You were drawing hop scotches on your drive in chalk and drinking
home-made lemonade.
Playing childish games like hide-and-seek and British bulldog.
Where did your outdoor games evaporate to?

When was it when you were playing outdoors on old bicycles
out on adventures?
When you were safe, when going out alone with your friends
was expected.
Why has so much changed?

After school when there was no homework to be done, skipping with
the neighbour's children
And even playing rounders together was normal.

Why have children changed so much?
Why have they become dependent on technology?
Have adults taught us wrong?
What has time done to change our delicate minds?
Somewhere among the thoughts of technology, we yearn for
freedom - how it used to be.
How can so much change in so little time?

Sophie Amanda Pearce (14)
Uplands School, Poole

In Time, I'm Sure

The thought of the first few words is chilling
But a soothing feeling comes around me
It's too late to turn around and run back
I have to face this sensibly or else
I could take a wrong turn and regret it.

You feel the same way too, like me, don't you?
Your face sends signs of truth and sympathy
Move on, stay calm but still the feelings show
It's gone already, I can see and now
Was this worth nothing or can we fix this
I'm sure it's not so bad but it's not straight.

You don't want to be here but I can see
It's me, isn't it, I should just give up
We don't stand a chance from where I see it
But it's you, your choice, tell me now or find
That I want this to be not then but now
And in return no one notices me.

It's easier when I'm not the person
To express the feelings I have for you
When it's talking and gazing at your smile
A sense of gratitude takes over me
I can't tell you how I feel because it's hard
I know you want to hear it, I'm so sorry.

So I guess this is it, you hate me now
Or will I ever be able to tell
Because I'm sure that you will understand
That the only time you will hear me say
Is when I'm not with the world or half gone
But you'll find out some day, in time I'm sure.

Ali Wilson (15)
Uplands School, Poole

My Generation

MP3s have taken over records,
Computers have improved.
We use wireless Internet.
We play on electric games consoles.
We watch satellite TV with a 50 inch flat screen.

Temperature is rising slowly due to global warming
Ice glaciers are melting quickly
Many animals are dying
We can stop it if we stop using our luxuries.

We go abroad a lot because of jets and aeroplanes
We are getting obese because of lack of exercise
Supermarkets are taking over little shops
Then they will make more profit.

Cars are extremely powerful now
They can go over 100mph
We use carbon fibre which makes us go faster
Fuel costs are £1 a litre.

Old buildings are being demolished
To make way for flats
Population has increased
There are now 6.6 billion people in the world
Britain is now overcrowded.

This is what is happening in my generation.

Joseph Krolski (14)
Uplands School, Poole

My Changing World

I was born 12-3-93
This makes me 14½
My generation has more,
More choice
More TV
More food
More DVDs and magazines
More sports to try
More restrictions
Too much traffic to ride my bike
Too much food to eat in the fridge.

In my generation England won the Rugby World Cup
Can we do it again?
No one else has won twice
England won the Ashes
The world is getting warmer
Floods
Droughts
Muddled seasons
But no more hurricanes.

Mobile phones to keep in touch
PlayStations to drive, ski, shoot or kill
How did Mum and Dad survive without a PC
The Internet
And me!

Jack Abrahams (14)
Uplands School, Poole

Hello Korea (Or Somewhere Like That)

The Internet connects me
To someone in a far-off region
I will probably never meet them
Yet we talk as if we are ten kilometres from each other.

I've got Kasabian,
Kaiser Chiefs, White Stripes
And many more on a little piece of plastic
As thin as a pencil.

Don't say brainstorm
That was a close one.
A few phrases we can't say
Because people are offended.

In fifty years we're all going to die
According to all those brainy types.
(think about it, Ali G)
Cos global warming is, like, making ice caps melt.

You knows?
Aieeet?
Boom, shake da room
And all that jazz.

Am I still making sense
Or am I just babbling.
I'm probably boring you
Or something like that.

Now, what's on the tube?

Edward Parker (13)
Uplands School, Poole

Individualism

Nike, French Connection, Dolce & Gabbana
Are all these little labels us?
Do we have nothing but these names?
Are we labelled by a factory outlet?
Is he Nike, is she Dolce & Gabbana?

Is that boy with the long hair, is he Converse?
Is that girl with the short hair, is she Etnies?
Are we meant to hate him because he wears Converse?
Are we meant to hate her because she wears Etnies?

Or is that boy John?
Is that girl just called Susan?
So I ask you, do you hate people for their labels?
Is being yourself a crime?

Do you take pride in yourself?
Can you say, I wear what I want and I don't care what you think!
Or will you be the one who discriminates people for what they are?
I think bravery isn't trying something new with your hair
I think bravery is going out of the door and not caring
what people think!

Tom Hawkins (15)
Uplands School, Poole

What's it All About?

What's this generation all about?
Are we really 'bovered'?
We all want fame and fortune,
We all want the spotlight,
But we don't know why.
Girls want to be 'WAGS',
Boys want to be footballers.
What's it all about?

Gone are the days of innocent play,
Out come the knives, where the stakes are high.
Peer pressure grows like a runaway train,
Soon it's a monster out of control.
What's it all about?

Is money making us happy
Or is it the root of all evil?
Our grandparents talk of 'the good old days',
Where money was tight, but morals were high.

When *we* look back on *our* childhood memories,
Will *we* be proud to call these
'The good old days'?

Georgie Rowbrey (13)
Uplands School, Poole

Technology

As I sit on my bed I reflect
On the photo album in my hands
Many photographs of happy people
Stare at me from the pages
One photo stands out
My grandad as a young boy
Playing with a yo-yo and string.
I now look at my new Xbox
All the technology surrounding me is amazing
He never had these privileges
My mobile phone, my iPod, and TV
All these I take for granted
And now I see how lucky I am
And for once appreciate what is given to me
I now imagine the future
And what generations to come will have
As my grandfather, I may never see these
All I can hope is my grandchildren
And theirs as well
Will appreciate as I now do
The technology surrounding them.

Melissa Ward (13)
Uplands School, Poole

And We Know . . .

We have television
A portal into other worlds.
Whether people have created them,
Or if nature's hands have shaped them.
We have the Internet
And can speak with other worlds
We may choose to help them
Or only walk away.

And we know . . .

We can travel quickly,
And fast we cover ground.
It may not cost us much
But there is a price to pay.
As I travel forward I talk to those at home
Even if there's no one else nearby.

And we know . . .

But all of what we know,
And most of what we have
We could never ever have had
If it wasn't for those before us.
If we were the first ones,
(and we most certainly weren't)
We would have been the ones to invent
All of the things we have now
Years and years ago.

And we know . . .

I wonder what we'll do to help the human race.
Will we help at all, I wonder
Will the future generation benefit from us
Or will they only know what we know?

Joanna Tonge (13)
Uplands School, Poole

Today's Generation

Technology has taken over
Everywhere you look you can see the future.

Massive flatscreens, iPods, computers
Year by year it increases.

Phones are very important
It may be to some people.

Years ago there wasn't any technology
Like we have now.

Not all people around the world
Have the same equipment and technology that we have.

Show some mercy
Towards them

Respect what you have
Respect the people around you.

Tishco Gurdji (14)
Uplands School, Poole

Dreaming, Believing

The stars seem so bright tonight
Maybe it's your eyes that seem to gleam tonight
Or maybe it's because you're with me tonight
All I can say is that tonight you're with me
Although tomorrow I know that you'll be with some other guy
So why are you here wasting both of our times
When you could be at home chatting up some other guy?
So why don't you leave and never say goodbye
Or maybe that sparkle in your eyes is because you really
                                           do love me?
So goodbye for now my love for tomorrow I shall return to this
                                           very same dream

To see you face yonder with me
Or maybe tomorrow you'll be with some other guy.
As there is no certainty with the uncertainty of love.

James Marlowe
Uplands School, Poole

Change

Haven't things changed?
No more black and white photos
Or small corner shops
Where all household products could be bought!
Nowadays we have huge supermarkets
That tower over all other shops
Like an evil wizard casting
Shadows over each person.

Whatever happened to the typical happy family
With a mum, a dad and kids?
Why is it that children are abandoned
Or one parent is left to raise their child alone?
What is this obsession that
Wanting to achieve more is wrong?
Going out in clothes that leave
Nothing to the imagination.

What has happened to our world?
Where has the regular person gone?
Who doesn't feel the need to impress.
Why can't we all be as we once were?
. . . because change is what we do best!

India De Silva Jeffries (13)
Uplands School, Poole

As I Sit Here Alone

As I sit here alone in the local park,
Listening to my new pink iPod,
Justin Timberlake's new song's playing.

I can hear a tune,
My jeans' pocket lights up,
My phone's ringing.
I'm expecting this call,
It's getting late,
I'm all alone.

As I slowly walk home,
Teenagers start shouting at me,
I am scared,
I see them with bottles of alcohol,
What should I do?

It's cold,
Squeals and squeaks come round the corner,
I hear a gunshot,
I drop to the floor with a thump.

Katherine Charman (13)
Uplands School, Poole

My England

This is my England, this is my hometown
In every playground a druggie waits
Kids left to fend, but where are the parents?
Murders, stabbings, who cares?

This is my England, this is my hometown
Society split down the middle
Chavs, emos, goths and the rest all at war
But those in power don't care.

This is my England, this is my hometown
PC has gone too far
You can't say black sheep, that's too much
English people can't be English.

This is my England, this is my hometown
England has become new Europe
The economy can't cope with more scroungers
But for those who work we welcome with open arms.

Rob Booth (13)
Uplands School, Poole

Brands

We go to school with our branded bags
We write with our branded pencils
Not a thought goes for how they're made
We laugh and smile with all our glee
Free-dress day would suddenly arrive
What we are wearing matters so much
Best shoes, best top and sunglasses too
We are all clones of the branding industry
It used to be that you couldn't write
Now plastic rather than feathers
We flick ink without giving a second thought
For how we are wasting something important
Appreciation of standards just fades away
I now they knew what it was like then
They would wear that for the sake of it
Hypocritical as am I
I feel it's my duty to convey
The reality of the brand industry.

Will Brown (15)
Uplands School, Poole

My Life Is Simple Compared To Others

As I walk down the road, I listen to my music.
I text my friends on my swanky new mobile.
I get my wallet out to check I have money.
My life is simple, compared to others.

I've just bought a new watch, stylish some might say.
I've ordered some new games on the Internet.
I've bought a new pair of jeans to keep up with the trends.
My life is simple, compared to others.

I have hot and cold water just by turning a tap.
I have hot food just by heating an oven.
I press a switch and *bang!* the light is on
My life is simple, compared to others.

My parents always tell me, 'You wouldn't get that in my day'
I usually just ignore them, and carry on playing my Xbox.
I suppose, when I think about it, they're right.
My life is simple, compared to others.

Timothy Johnson (15)
Uplands School, Poole

Parents Just Don't Understand

Mum didn't allow us,
We were desperate to play on the Nintendo Wii,
I'd presently bought this new game you know,
Parents just don't understand.

I just received a text from my mate,
'Oh, is that the radio?'
'No Mum, it's my mobile!'
Parents just don't understand.

'Oh I wonder what the score was of the final tennis open.'
'Just go on teletext Dad!'
'What's that?' he replied having no clue . . .
Parents just don't understand.

'Complete you homework!' they both said.
'I am, I am!' I informed them for the fifth time.
'No you're not, you're on the computer.'
Parents just don't understand.

Toby Khalife
Uplands School, Poole

Talkin' 'Bout My Generation

It's the 21st century,
The technology is great,
All hi-tech and futuristic,
Where did all those years go?

Lots more gadgets and gismos,
Like iPods and MP3s,
Photoshops and digi-cameras,
And mobile phones galore.

We all love our laptops,
And our PCs too,
But think about all the others,
Who don't have as much as we have.

When the day is over,
I realise how fast they're changing,
The old days are now memories,
To dwell on and remember.

Jamie Everett (12)
Uplands School, Poole

Aeroplane

I am in an aeroplane
Flying through the sky
Leaving trails where I go
Blue, white and red.
I'm rather loud
As I fly up and down,
Around and around.
My outside is hard and smooth
But inside I am soft and comforting.
As I prepare to fly
Back to my base,
I see the crowd, thousands at most
But as I land on the ground
I think to myself.
My time is over
In my red and white
Fast little plane.

Peter Jeff (14)
Uplands School, Poole

Young Writers Information

We hope you have enjoyed reading this book - and that you will continue to enjoy it in the coming years.

If you like reading and writing poetry drop us a line, or give us a call, and we'll send you a free information pack.

Alternatively if you would like to order further copies of this book or any of our other titles, then please give us a call or log onto our website at www.youngwriters.co.uk

Young Writers Information
Remus House
Coltsfoot Drive
Peterborough
PE2 9JX

(01733) 890066